MW01503758

One
in Year
Politics

A Politics Project by Morgan Searcy

One Year in Politics

Published by Morgan Searcy LLC.

Copyright (c) 2023, Morgan Searcy.
First edition, published 2023.

Editor: **Amy Schubert**
Data and project support: **Irina Alejandro**
Reviewed by: **Raquel Breternitz**, **Kiayna O'Neal**,
Colleen Murphy, and **Tim Norton**

All rights reserved. No parts of the publication may be
reproduced or transmitted in any form or by any means,
electronic or mechanical, including photocopy, recording
or any information storage and retrieval system, without
prior permission in writing from the publisher.

Every reasonable attempt has been made to
identify owners of copyright. Errors or omissions
will be corrected in subsequent editions.

ISBN: 979-8-9887466-0-7
eISBN: 979-8-9887466-1-4

Design: Morgan Searcy
Cover image: Spurekar
Printed and bound in USA

from first-time
Democratic staffers
in the 2020 cycle

politicsproject.com

Morgan Searcy

Introduction
from the author

I was raised in a home and community that didn't openly talk about politics. When I was young, I remember prying my parents for their opinions on current events and ending up mostly empty-handed. So, in some ways, it surprises me to be here opening a report on improving Democratic campaigns and political spaces. But on the other hand, I found myself free from a young age to form values outside my environment.

Growing up Asian-American in the notoriously conservative state of Alabama helped me recognize the disconnect between my forming beliefs and those of many of my peers. As a shy senior in my public school AP government class, feminism felt radical. Celebrating marriage equality was taboo. Funding government programs 'undermined' hard-working 'American' values of the popular kids.[1]

I felt disconnected from what I wanted to believe and those around me. After several summers outside of Alabama while studying graphic design in college, I wondered what would happen if the efforts of corporate branding and design would be applied to support legislation or progressive values. If people could visualize and understand the flaws of the American healthcare system, immediacy of climate change, or steps to prison reform, change would be easier; right?

In the fall of 2019, I gratefully joined *Warren for President*. There I quickly saw the benefits and hurdles of political campaigns as temporary structures. There was a remarkable level of dedication from each person on the campaign—all working in systems practically created overnight. Once a candidate is no longer a viable option or the election is over, typically, the campaign's resources and insights disappear quickly. Not having efficient or accessible means to share the direct experiences and insights gained during a cycle felt like an oversight in the work, progress, and efforts of campaigns.

Being a part of Jon Ossoff's runoff campaign led me to work with a lot of young people with experience from two or more other campaigns and/or organizations that were directly involved in the cycle. The runoff campaign was an example of successfully organizing and shifting resources from primaries starting in mid-2019 to a 2020 November general election and onward to two January 2021 Senate runoff races.

---

1. Democratic values which many of my ex-classmates who have moved out of state now support.

The 2020 Georgia runoffs felt unique, as the two Senate campaigns and supporting organizations had the infrastructure and access to recruit both local and remote staffers and volunteers. The newly assembled, top-tier teams sprinted with their experiences of both winning and losing Democratic races from across the country.

And so, in Georgia, there was a deeper understanding of how to approach the election, from campaign systems to on-the-ground and remote organizing strategies. The lengthy 2020 cycle allowed staffers to gain and pass down knowledge nationwide—giving the Democratic Party an edge in Georgia.

As I was wrapping up with my team in Georgia, everyone had handfuls of specific knowledge from their work. Entry and mid-level peers had access to test new methods while also concepting and running whole programs. Some campaign staffers take to social media or their inner circles to debrief, there is no standard for closing and retaining knowledge from campaigns and election-based organizations. Retaining insights for future use is an informal and often inaccessible process. As the cycle closed in early 2021, I watched my co-worker's experiences fade.

Concluding the 2020 cycle, there were more examples of staffers independently working together to document their processes (e.g. *Emma Friend*'s debrief of Ed Markey 2020's relational-first organizing approach[2], and Jon Ossoff's Digital Organizing Director, *Davis Lenord's* breakdown of building relational networks[3]). Both of these women-led knowledge-sharing projects required unpaid labor for the good of the progressive movement.

One Year in Politics uses research and design to respond to the short-term nature of campaign systems that prevents accessible institutional knowledge to support more sustainable and effective practices.

In this research, when referring to "first-time staffers," I am specifically referring to individuals who have recently entered the workforce and political work. Electoral spaces include and thrive from many who have switched industries or professions into politics. However, I wanted the ability to narrow in on a specific demographic when collecting stories.

I used my access and experience as a first-time staffer on *Warren for President* in 2020 and *Jon Ossoff for Senate*'s reelection campaign to define this demographic. Focusing on this group of staffers also allowed for similar life milestones as they were approaching politics and work for the first time.

Recently graduated, first-time staffers also provide a look into Gen Z's participation trends and insight into future Party and movement leaders. In 2020, campaign managers, on average, were aged 41, with typically eight Senate cycles and four presidential cycles under their belts.[4] It was also reported that the age of local and state campaign leadership was trending younger in 2020.[5]

My hope is that we, the Party and the progressive movement more broadly, will create more efficient systems to retain and exchange knowledge among staffers and volunteers. Transparency within campaign spaces will benefit future recruitment and retention of those supporting the movement. Leveraging past experiences allows for more efficient and future-focused approaches to cyclical campaign work.

—Morgan Searcy

2. Friend, E., Clark, R., Thibodeau, J., Kent, J. (2020, September 22). *Ed Markey's relational-first organizing approach.* https://medium.com/@emma.h.friend/ed-markeys-relational-first-organizing-approach-137bbfc4852

3. Leonard, D., Stein, Z., & Kravitz, J. (2022, April 11). *How we built a relational network of 160K voters in less than a month.* https://medium.com/@davisleonard/how-we-built-a-relational-network-of-160k-voters-in-less-than-a-month-92262926fdb0

4. *Campaign manager demographics and statistics [2023]: Number of campaign managers in the US.* Campaign Manager Demographics and Statistics [2023]: Number Of Campaign Managers In The US. (2022, September 9). https://www.zippia.com/campaign-manager-jobs/demographics

5. Bograd, S. (2020, October 28). *Recent college grads are running political campaigns.* Teen Vogue. https://www.teenvogue.com/story/campaign-managers-state-local-elections

One Year *in* Politics

225 First Time Staffers. 40 interviews.

All were directly involved in the 2020 election cycle.

The initial call for this report's participants began January 25, 2021 via Twitter and was shared through other networks.

Among 225 first-time staffers, a total of *415 different jobs* with 150 different employers was reported. Many of these people took on multiple positions within the cycle, with a few holding five different roles in 2020.

40 recently graduated individuals shared what it was like working in politics for the first time by answering twelve open-ended questions.

415
Jobs Held.

53% with a campaign.

26% with the Democratic party.

21% with an Organization.

150 Total Employers.

Out of the reported roles, *53%* were within campaigns, the remaining positions were with Democratic Party efforts[6] *(26%)*, and organizations[7] directly involved *in* the 2020 cycle *(21%)*.

Collectively, their campaign experience represents 43 congressional, 13 state, 11 presidential, *and* 8 local candidates.

---

6. Democratic Party efforts are being defined as state Democratic Parties and efforts such as *'Texas Democratic Party'* and *'Maine Democratic Party Coordinated Campaign'.*

7. Organization efforts include any group that is not directly related to a campaign or the Democratic Party but is doing work directly related to voter turnout or the election. Eg. *'One Campaign for Michigan'* or *'When We All Vote.'*

All *quotes* and *interviews* were collected between January 2021 and April 2021. Quotes have been lightly edited for clarity.

Motivations of First-Time Staffers *in* 2020

The intense political energy lingering from 2016 helped set the tone for the 2020 presidential election cycle in the United States. Throughout the country, many people searched for more equitable and just representations in their government. 2020 felt like a rare moment with the potential to hold historical significance. Democrats and progressives were energized. Voters were ready. Young people wanted to get involved.

These recently graduated young adults saw the cycle as an opportunity for *progress* and political reform. Their political consciousness and priorities helped motivate them to *seek change*.

Unlike the previous presidential election cycle, dominated only by a few Democratic candidates, the 2020 presidential primary saw the largest number of candidates in the party's history.[8] Voters had a broad selection of presidential candidate options with more than twenty-five major Democratic campaigns. 2020 helped voters, especially young people, to identify candidates best aligned with their values and beliefs.

8. The Economist Newspaper. (n.d.). *Who is ahead in the Democratic primary race?*. The Economist. https://projects.economist.com/democratic-primaries-2020

I knew to *bring change,* I would have to put in the work.

Natalie Valenzuela
One APIA Nevada

On Election Night in 2016, my dad called me crying and said he felt he was back in Apartheid-era South Africa (where he's from). That struck a chord with me, and I remember thinking, 'okay, when I graduated in 2020, Trump's first term will be up—*I have to be a part of that.*'

Hannah Ezell
Kansas Democratic Party

I was terrified of another four years of Donald Trump. I turned down *multiple full-time* job offers to work on a campaign that resonated with me.

Anonymous Staffer
Warren for President

I had been waiting for the 2020 elections for years. Not only was [this] our chance to get rid of Donald Trump, but it was also a chance to *build progressive power* and elect people who would work to fight the crises we're facing at the scales which they demand. As a young person, I feel the weight of the climate crisis and the urgency with which we must act.

The 2020 elections signified a turning point and a decisive moment in history, and I knew I wanted to be part of it.

Gabbi Perry
Alex Morse for Congress / Michigan Democratic Party

These young people were ready to contribute and make a positive impact with campaigns and political organizations gearing up for the 2020 presidential election cycle.

As their chosen candidates dropped out of the primary, they reconciled their losses and often shifted their dedication to the remaining viable campaigns. Their vision was for a better version of the country through elected officials.

Shared Experiences
Led to Involvement

Understanding the involvement of our interviewees in the 2020 presidential cycle requires recognizing the significance of cultural and historical events they have experienced in the past decade in America. Most of the interviewees split the line between the Millennial generation, which championed the Obama and Clinton campaigns, and the new digital generation of Gen Z.[9,10]

This group of young people were raised by parents without smartphones but were also among the first to define social media. These staffers represent a generation of children that grew up with the effects of Columbine and 9/11 while witnessing Sandy Hook as elementary children. As preteens, they watched the Obamas enter the White House. Over eight years of his administration, these young people saw the President's views evolve, leading to legislation and stances that they held pride in.

As technology develops quicker, there becomes a larger gap in experiences between the beginning, middle and end of the traditional ten year generations. Identifying generations by decades, as commonly done, ignores the core characteristics of political cohorts.

Micro-generations, or the distinct characteristics of individuals within the conventional generational decade timeframe, can provide better insight into people's motivations and habits. Understanding the experiences of different micro-generations allows the Party and movement to identify groups of staffers (or voters) more individually rather than placing broad generalizations on them.[11] Each election cycle gives new opportunities for first-time voters and fresh staff members to enter the space. The first-time staffers of 2020 represent a micro-generation between millennials and Gen Z. They had exposure to online conversations and ideas beyond their households, communities, and even country, which led them to discover and understand their truths about America.

9. Kirby , E. H., & Kawashima-Ginsberg, K. (2019, August 17). *The Youth Vote in 2008* . Youth on the Trail 2012. http://www.whatkidscando.org/youth.on.the.trail.2012/pdf/IOP.Voters.Guide.pdf

10. Dimock, M. (2023, May 11). *Defining generations: Where millennials end and generation Z begins.* Pew Research Center. https://www.pewresearch.org/fact-tank/2019/01/17/where-millennials-end-and-generation-z-begins

11. Whittier, N. (1997). *Political Generations, Micro-Cohorts, and the Transformation of Social Movements.* American Sociological Review, 62(5), 760–778. https://doi.org/10.2307/2657359

This timeline, starting in 1995, represents some of the cultural events and nuances that played a role in shaping the cohort of recently graduated, first-time staffers in the 2020 election cycle.

General milestones from interviewees are marked to help contextualize the influences of these events with their coming-of-age and interest in Democratic politics. Note these are only the experiences of some, not all of the interviewees.

1995

The Oklahoma City bombings.

Michael Jordan returns to the NBA after ending his retirement.

U.S. aides Mexico's economy with $20-billion aid program.

eBay is launched.

150 million people watch the O.J. Simpson's not-guilty verdict.

1996

U.S. Presidential Election year, Bill Clinton and Al Gore win against Bob Dole & Jack Kemp.

MSNBC, a 24hr news channel, is launched in partnership with Microsoft and NBC.

The Summer Olympics are in Atlanta, Georgia.

1997

Cloning of Dolly the sheep.

The first Harry Potter book is published.

Princess Diana's death.

1998

Clinton-Lewinsky scandal breaks.

Apple announces the iMac.

The search engine, *Google*, is released to the internet.

1999

Eleven countries initiated the use of the Euro for their currency.

Columbine High School shooting in Littleton, Colorado.

Urban Dictionary was created.

President Bill Clinton faces impeachment proceedings.

Y2K bug in computers.

2000

U.S. Presidential Election year, George Bush and Dick Cheney win against Al Gore after Florida recounts.

The Sims is released.

NASA reports the hole in the Ozone layer over Antarctica increased by .62 sq miles to 17 square miles in 12 months.

Wikipedia, a free content encyclopedia, goes online.

2001

No Child Left Behind Act,
education bill passed.

Shrek is released.

September 11 attacks in
New York City.

The U.S. launches an
invasion of Afghanistan.

The Patriot Act is established.

—
Cohort starts kindergarten

2002

The Department of Homeland
Security is created in response
to September 11.

Space Shuttle Columbia
disintegrates upon re-entry,
resulting in a 29-month
suspension of the Space
Shuttle program.

The Euro becomes the official
currency of 12 of the European
Union's members.

Salt Lake City, Utah hosts
the Winter Olympics.

2003

Myspace and itunes are released.

Human Genome Project
sequences 99% of the genome.

Finding Nemo enters theaters.

Unemployment peaks at 6.3%.

Saddam Hussein is captured
by U.S. forces.

2004

U.S. Presidential Election Year, George Bush and Dick Cheney win against John Kerry and John Edwards.

Facebook becomes open to the general public.

Last episode of *Friends* airs while *The Incredibles* and *Mean Girls* are in theaters.

Environmental protection laws dropped to allow increased logging in US National Forests. Facebook becomes open to the general public.

Environmental protection laws dropped to allow increased logging in US National Forests.

2005

The Kyoto Protocol, to reduce global emissions, goes into effect, without U.S. support.

Launch of Youtube, Webkinz and Club Penguin.

First generation iPod Nano & Xbox 360 released.

Hurricane Katrina hits states on the Gulf of Mexico.

The first book in the *Twilight* saga is published.

2006

Twitter is founded.

Taylor Swift releases her debut album.

TSA implemented heightened security measures, including banning all liquids.

Google buys YouTube.

Nintendo Wii release before the holiday shopping season.

2007

Nancy Pelosi becomes the women Speaker of the U.S. House of Reps.

Netflix streaming began.

The iPhone & iPod touch are announced.

The 2000s recession *officially* begins in December.

—
Begins middle school

2008

U.S. Presidential Election year, Barack Obama and Joe Biden win against John McCain and Sarah Palin.

A global financial crisis begins as the stock market crashes.

Beijing hosts the Summer Olympics.

2009

Barack Obama is sworn in as the first African-American President of the U.S.

The first of a series of Tea Party protests are conducted across the United States.

Just Dance was made exclusively for the Wii.

2010

A catastrophic earthquake hits Haiti, affecting 3M+ people.

The Healthcare Reform Bill and Affordable Care Act passes in Congress.

An oil rig explodes in the Gulf of Mexico, millions of gallons spill into the sea.

The Winter Olympics are held in Vancouver, Canada.

Instagram is founded.

SpaceX successfully launches a capsule and it returns from low-Earth orbit.

—
Enters high school

2011

U.S. Rep. Gabrielle Giffords is severely shot in an assassination attempt in suburban Tucson, Arizona.

Syria's civil war began.

The end of NASA's 30-year shuttle program.

Repealing of "Don't Ask, Don't Tell" policy.

The Royal Wedding between Kate Middleton and Prince William.

2012

Marvel's *The Avengers* is released and becomes one of the highest-grossing films.

Shooting at a midnight screening of *The Dark Knight Rises* in Aurora, Colorado.

The *Curiosity Rover* successfully lands on Mars.

Sandy Hook Elementary shooting happens in Connecticut.

Rihanna, Adele, Bruno Mars, Gotye, Carly Rae Jepsen, and Taylor Swift top the charts and win awards.

2013

The shooting of Michael Brown by a police officer occurs in Ferguson, MO.

Black Lives Matter movement starts.

Lance Armstrong admitted to doping in all of his *Tour de France* wins.

Vine is released.

—

Preparing for higher education opportunities with SAT and ACT testing

2014

The West African Ebola virus outbreak begins.

ALS Ice Bucket Challenge goes viral on social media.

The Winter Olympics is hosted in Sochi, Russia.

Janet Yellen becomes first woman to be the Chairperson of the Federal Reserve.

In an effort to reduce costs, high lead levels in water begin a crisis in Flint, Michigan.

U.S.-Cuba relations improve after decades of sanctions.

2015

Charlie Hebdo attacks killing journalists sparking the phrase *'Je Suis Charlie'*.

The Broadway's premiere of Lin-Manuel Miranda's *Hamilton* production.

Freddie Gray's murder at the hand of police sparks Baltimore protests.

The world agrees on a climate change deal with the *Paris Climate Accord*.

Charleston, South Carolina church shooting.

Marriage equality becomes legal in all 50 U.S. states after Supreme Court ruling.

The Refugee Crisis in Europe continues to grow.

San Bernardino shooting was the deadliest mass shooting since the 2012 in the U.S.

—

Begins higher education

2016

U.S. Presidential Election year, Donald Trump and Mike Pence win against Hillary Clinton and Tim Kaine.

The Zika virus becomes a health epidemic.

The continued threat of ISIS.

Increased national attention on the opioid crisis in the U.S.

Hillary Clinton becomes first woman nominee for president by a major political party in the U.S.

The murders of Alton Sterling and Philando Castile by police.

The UK votes to leave the EU.

Protests at Standing Rock and Dakota Access Pipeline.

Pulse nightclub shooting in Orlando, Florida.

Rio, Brazil hosts the Summer Olympics to backlash.

The Syrian refugee crisis continues in Europe.

Colin Kaepernick kneels.

Chicago Cubs win the *World Series* for the first time in 108 years.

Total number of BIPOC women in the Senate increases from one to four.

2017

Women's March in D.C.— the largest single-day protest in U.S. history.

The U.S. sets a travel ban on seven predominantly Muslim countries.

Margaret Atwood *Handmaid's Tale* is adapted to a TV show.

An investigation on Russia's involvement in the 2016 U.S. Presidential Election begins.

The President says there are *'very fine people on both sides'* of the white supremacist rally in Charlottesville, Virgina.

Las Vegas shooting becomes the deadliest mass shooting in modern U.S. history.

A solar eclipse passes over much of the U.S. sparking excitement.

The White House becomes frequent to a quick rotation of staff and leadership.

The beginning of the *#MeToo* movement is a result of NYT's reporting on Weinstein.

Record-setting hurricane season across the globe.

2018

Marjory Stoneman Douglas High School shooting happens in Parkland, Florida.

Meghan Markle joins the British royal family.

Dr. Christine Blasey Ford testifies before Kavanaugh's nomination to the Supreme Court.

Major retailers begin announcing bankruptcy (*Sears* and *Toys "R" Us*).

UN Intergovernmental Panel found that Earth will warm by 2.7°F by 2040.

Democrats take control of the House during a record turnout midterm election.

—

Graduating from school and entering the workforce

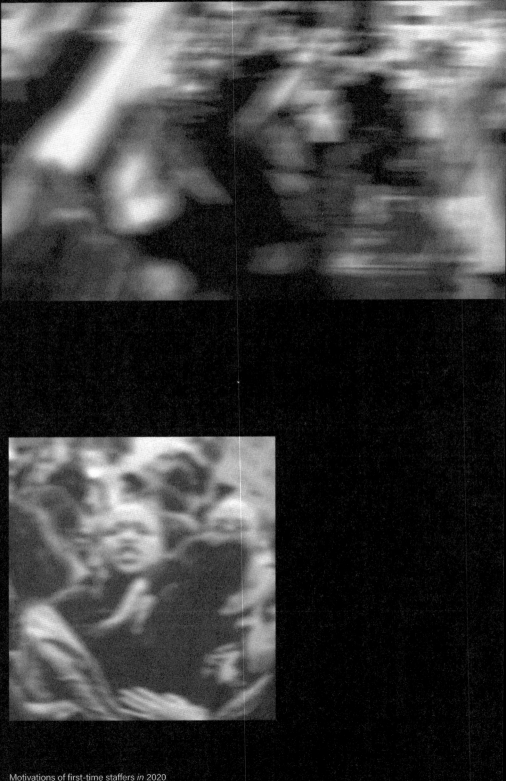

Motivations of first-time staffers *in* 2020

In the interviewees' eyes, the 2016 presidential election results hurt both them and their country. The policies and presence of the new administration were a threat to the daily lives of the people they cared about. They had a different vision of the future. After 2016, young adults continued joining together and building momentum. Efforts such as the Women's March in early 2017 led to growing political commitment and record youth turnout in the 2018 midterms.[12]

Most in this cohort graduated during or near the 2020 election year. They discovered double available jobs in electoral work compared to non-presidential election years.[13] Their increasing activism and the natural transitional period after graduation helped draw post-graduates to join the 2020 campaign as first-time staffers.

Once on campaigns, many recognized parts of themselves in their peers and young voters. These first-time staffers used their backgrounds and understanding of Democratic values to give new insights into voters while sharing their visions for the future.

12. Election night 2018: *Historically high youth turnout, support for Democrats.* Circle at Tufts. (2018, November 7). https://circle.tufts.edu/latest-research/election-night-2018-historically-high-youth-turnout-support-democrats

13. Gao, G. (2020, May 30). *The up and down seasons of political campaign work.* Pew Research Center. https://www.pewresearch.org/short-reads/2014/11/17/the-seasonal-nature-of-political-campaign-work

On the Availability of Recent Graduates

Having the freedom to be in short-term, high-risk jobs was the most common reason why first-time staffers got involved with the 2020 cycle. Among those interviewed, graduation years ranged from 2018 to the spring months of 2020. More than half (57.5%) of the 40 interviewees cited graduating *near* the cycle as a reason they became paid staffers in the 2020 cycle. These graduates, ranging from college to high school, had plans to support Democratic and progressive efforts in their cycle. Some first-time staffers even took breaks from their education to be involved first-hand.

2020 provided a lot of available roles for entry-level positions. The overflow of open roles and the tough job market enabled graduates to find numerous employment opportunities in Democratic politics. Recent graduates entering the middle of the 2020 cycle, during the beginning of the pandemic, found political campaign work as one of the few actively hiring spaces for recent graduates.

Although convenient, young adults' involvement in the 2020 cycle was not accidental. Many interviewees planned to be involved in some capacity for several years leading up to 2020. Graduation lining up with the presidential cycle became an opportunity to commit to their political ideologies.

Motivations for First-Time Staff's Involvement in the 2020 campaigns cycle
Top 5 reasons cited from interviews for their employment in 2020.

Graduation Year Aligned
57.5%

'High Stakes' of the Election Cycle
44.5%

A Specific Candidate
37.5%

Prospects for a Better Future
37.5%

The Results of 2016 Cycle/Present Administration
27.5%

Young people *often* have the flexibility to adapt to the demands of campaign life.

After the results of November 2016, Nelowfar Ahmadi, a graduate from the University of California at Riverside, switched majors that semester from engineering to public policy because she "wanted to get into the fight to combat anti-immigrant policies and Islamophobia that Trump and his supporters were pushing."

To Sonja Thrasher that being involved in the campaign trail was the "most important thing" she could do out of undergrad. Sonja, a 2019 graduate from the *University of California at Irvine*, felt that 2020 would be the election of her lifetime. Working directly in the election cycle was a clear post-graduation path for her and may of the interviewees.

With fewer established responsibilities, some people could effectively meet the demands of campaign life, leading to their participation in the 2020 campaign cycle. Many felt a sense of urgency to put aside their plans in order to be involved with the 2020 cycle.

Ongoing investments of paid opportunities are important for engagement of new perspectives in Democratic political spaces. Non-cyclical organizations and structures can contribute to the recruitment of the movement. The Democratic-led *Organizing Corps 2020'* hosted a paid training program that focused on "young people of color" that could support nationwide grassroots efforts during the presidential cycle.[14] Programs like Organizing Corps help lower the entry barrier in electoral spaces by reducing the learning curve and access to campaign jobs. Establishing relationships with prospective young staffers before important election years can create ongoing support for the Party's efforts.

14. The Democrats. (2019, February 21). *DNC Launches New Program: Organizing Corps 2020. Democrats News.* https://democrats.org/news/dnc-launches-new-program-organizing-corps-2020

First-time staffers were most likely to work with a Presidential race
The percentages of campaign roles in 2020 by category, (53% of total reported jobs).

Presidential Campaigns

45.5%

Senate Campaigns

28%

U.S. House Campaigns

17.5%

House Campaigns

7%

Local Campaigns

5%

Presidential Campaigns Represented
Amy for America, Bernie 2020, Beto for America,
Biden for President, Cory 2020, Gillibrand 2020,
Kamala Harris for The People, Mike Bloomberg 2020,
Pete for America, Tom Steyer 2020, Warren for President.

Senate Candidates Represented
Adrian Perkins (LA), Amy McGrath (KT), Charles Booker (KT), Doug Jones (AL),
Ed Markey (MA), John Hickenlooper (CO), Jon Ossoff (GA), Jaime Harrison (SC),
Jeff Merkley (OR), Jon Ossoff (GA), Mark Kelly (AZ), Mike Espy (MS),
Sara Gideon (ME), Theresa Greenfield (IA), Tina Smith (NM), Raphael Warnock (GA).

House Candidates Represented
Dr. Al Gross (AK), Alex Morse (MA), Andrew Ferguson (GA),
Anthony Brindisi (NY), Ben McAdams (UT), Bryan Berghoef (MI),
Brynne Kennedy (MA),Candace Valenzuela (TX), Carolyn Bourdeaux (GA),
Cindy Axne (IA), Colin Allred (TX), Desiree Tims (OH), George Scott (PA),
Dr. Hiral Tipirneni (AZ), Jake Auchincloss (MA), Jessica Cisneros (TX),
Julie Oliver (TX), Kara Eastman (NE), Lauren Underwood (IL),
Ben McAdams (UT), Jerry McNerney (CA), Shannon Freshour (OR),
Sri Kulkarni (TX), Stephanie Murphy (FL), Susie Lee (NV), Tom Malinowski (NJ).

Local Candidates Represented
Chad Klitzman, Supervisor of Elections (FL); Chris Nettles, City Council (TX);
Danny Ceisler, District Attorney (PA); N/A, City Council District (TX);
Jack Kerfoot, City Council (OR); Joe McAnarney, County Commissioner (FL);
Michelle De La Isla, Mayor (KS); Noelita Lugo, School Board (TX).

These campaigns and candidates are only the ones openly credited by
participants. For example, some employers, such as 'PA Congressional
Campaign', were not included in this list above but were included in the total
numbers of employers or job category breakdowns.

When considering the experiences of recently graduated, first-time campaign staffers, it is crucial to acknowledge the barriers of entry into these roles. Putting first and last deposits down on rent in a new location with the uncertainty of how long you are there for is one of the risks all staffers must consider.

Many hired campaign staffers benefit from their access to educational backgrounds, experiences, and their ability to navigate high-risk, short-term employment. Not all young people have equal access to these opportunities. Privilege affects the pool of prospective staffers in the field.

The availability of young people to participate in campaign cycles often depends on their ability to engage with high-risk, short-term employment while navigating the financial implications of moving for work without relocation support.

Election cycles heavily depend on campus environments to reach young voters. When campuses shut down in 2020, organizers and campaigns had to work on ways to connect with young adults outside of universities. In response, teams ran targeted paid media ads to attract individuals for open roles for a larger in-community talent reach. For future cycles, it would be beneficial for campaigns and organizations to expand their outreach to other environments, given that 38% of young people do not continue education after high school graduation.[15]

The barriers to entry into campaign life—whether it is having internal connections, financial constraints, or education— affect the diversity of campaign staffers. Finding new ways to engage and include new perspectives in the Democratic Party process is important.

15. U.S. Bureau of Labor Statistics. (2022, May 23). *61.8 percent of recent high school graduates enrolled in college in October 2021*. TED: The Economics Daily. https://www.bls.gov/opub/ted/2022/61-8-per-cent-of-recent-high-school-graduates-enrolled-in-college-in-october-2021.htm#:-:text=Bureau%20of%20Labor%20Statistics%2C%20U.S.,visited%20April%2028%2C%202023).

Similar Ideologies &
the Crowded Primary

Candidates down the ballot attract young staffers by presenting attainable visions for their futures. In 2020, the candidates in the Democratic presidential primary gave young people a wide range of options. This variety of campaigns allowed these individuals to familiarize themselves with the series of messaging across the Democratic Party. First-time staffers in 2020 had more options than previous cycles to engage with a platform that aligned with their political ideologies.

The individual candidates of 2020 had a meaningful influence on recruiting first-time campaign staffers. We found 37.5% of the first-time staffers cited a specific candidate as a reason for their involvement in the cycle. Making room for individual candidates to inspire and influence the Party helps support initial recruitment efforts in a cycle leading to a larger staff pool going into a general election. The large 2020 primary field, notable for multiple women candidates, influenced many entry-level staffers who became managers later in the cycle.

One interviewee mentioned that she had set plans to work in the 2020 presidential cycle. So in college, she took opportunities to be involved in Democratic politics through volunteer and internship roles. The invaluable mentors she gained continued her interest in the race. This staffer was increasingly excited to see more women enter the presidential race; she knew in the back of her mind she wanted to work for a woman. As the race unfolded, she noticed that she started identifying with Elizabeth Warren as she spoke. From that point, this staffer started searching for opportunities to join *Warren for President*.

Hazel Rosenblum-Sellers found herself drawn to the 2020 election cycle because 'so many candidates' presented a unique opportunity, especially for women like her, to participate in a historic political moment. As a student, Rosenblum-Sellers had interned for Senator Harris and developed a strong admiration for her. Hazel packed up begin organizing in Iowa for *Kamala Harris for The People* a month after graduating in May 2019.

"I would wrap up my undergraduate degree and it would be *another* presidential election. 2020 felt like perfect timing."

Anonymous
Arizona field organizer

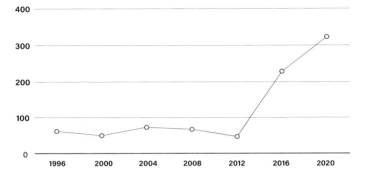

Registered Democratic Presidential Candidates, 1996-2020
The following chart shows a historical comparison of Democratic presidential candidates who filed with the FEC.[16, 17]

More than a third (37.5%) of first-time staffers got involved because of their hopes for a better future. *Warren for President* and *Ed Markey for Senate* fellow to organizer Ellen Smith "always had the drive to make the world a better place." When the election cycle came around, it was natural that she "jumped at the chance" to be a part of these two Boston-based campaigns. Like Ellen, other interviewees were change-focused, hoping to support a better future. Helping elect a specific candidate representing their values felt like a tangible and immediate path toward their visions.

This choice of who they worked for mattered to these first-time staffers. Like many American voters who express frustration for compromising on supporting a candidate on the ballot, young staffers found it difficult to align with a campaign. There was a significant disconnect between the Democratic platform and the political ideologies of young staffers. Among our interviewees, a majority (70%) were *unsure* if the campaign or organizations they worked for represented or aligned their political beliefs. While these young people were eager to support the efforts of the Democratic Party in 2020, working for campaigns that did not match their ideologies was difficult on personal and professional levels.

16. *Presidential candidates, 2020*. Ballotpedia. (n.d.). https://ballotpedia.org/Presidential. candidates,2020

17. *List of registered 2020 presidential candidates*. Ballotpedia. (n.d.-a). https://ballotpedia. org-List.of.registered.2020.presidential.candidates#cite.note-6

Young adults *focus* on change for a better future.

Nevertheless, almost 70% were *unsure* if their employer(s) represented their *beliefs.*

Hannah Gaffney, who worked on a local Arizona House race explained, "the district I worked in was primarily older, conservative white retirees and young, religious families so my candidates had to cater to those beliefs." She respected the campaign was true to the constituents' values. However, it wasn't easy to completely set aside her beliefs while working on the Arizona campaign.

In the middle of the campaign cycle and summer of 2020, George Floyd was murdered by a police officer in Minneapolis, Minnesota. Despite social distancing in effect for a global pandemic, much of the world came together to remember George Floyd around the world. Hannah explained, "It was *difficult* to publicly support 'truly moderate' candidates who didn't make public statements about pressing and socially relevant issues, like Black Lives Matter and gun control."

In the short term, separations between staffers and messaging lead to higher rates of burnout and mistrust in Democratic platforms, which can impact a staffers' enthusiasm for the work. Field organizer Michael Watson entered the 2020 primaries with a fairly moderate political stance, which aligned with his first campaign job on *Biden for President*. He shared that he was in "fairly close alignment" with the Biden campaign and policies when signing on. As the cycle progressed, opportunities for guaranteed employment pushed him to engage with *Bloomberg 2020*. Michael reflected that although "Bloomberg didn't really represent most [of] anything that I believe in, I took that job because the people hiring were promising employment through November." He explained his first priority was employment so the Bloomberg campaign seemed like "the best move" at the time.

Post-2020, Michael admitted that taking a job for short-term employment security *"was a mistake."* The Bloomberg campaign recruited staff from other campaigns by promising stability to the end of the election and offering almost double the pay as other campaigns.[16] This created a desirable option for some young people still figuring out themselves on their first job and their first-time in politics.

Quickly realizing that he did not align with Bloomberg 2020's campaign, Michael moved to support a couple of Democrats in local Idaho races. He found more shared general values with the two Idaho-based candidates, but learned "it's impossible to exactly agree on every issue." Michael noted, "The only time I was actually bothered by the policies of someone I was working for was the month working for Bloomberg."

16. Marsh, J. (2020, January 22). Here's how Mike Bloomberg is luring 2020 campaign staffers with lavish perks. New York Post. https://nypost.com/2020/01/22/heres-how-mike-bloomberg-is-luring-2020-campaign-staffers-with-lavish-perks

45% of first-time staffers *wished* their employers represented more *progressive* values.

Aligning common beliefs is important in choosing a campaign or organization to work for. Those who tried to match their values to the campaigns they worked on tended to have better experiences. At the end of 2020, 45% of interviewees wished the campaigns and organizations they worked for better aligned their personal, more progressive, political views. Young staffers' exposure to political work and their growing understanding of Democratic policy seemed to support *more* liberal views.

Like some of his peers, Michael shifts towards more progressive political stances throughout the cycle. He commented that he "went through a massive ideological shift over the course of the cycle." After the November 2020 election, he felt "far more progressive" than the Biden campaign.

An interviewee who worked as an organizer in Arizona before joining Georgia's Senate run-off races in January of 2021 shared her perspective of working with two campaigns with differing policy stances. She mentioned that while she respected her campaign's moderate approaches in Arizona, she was excited to join Jon Ossoff's campaign because the messaging aligned more closely with her beliefs. She felt the difference between working with the Senate campaign as "freeing" and more "empowering" because the messaging more closely aligned with the values she supported.

There is a strong desire for conversation, accountability, and change from young people. Staffers' trust grew when there was the opportunity for dialogue and changing perspectives. Helping staffers find campaigns that closely match their beliefs will help create better experiences at both ends.

Staffers' Ideological Differences With Employers
First-time staffers in 2020 across the board questioned the ideological differences between them and their employers, showing a difference in hope for more progressive values.

Percent mentioned unsure if their employer(s) represented their beliefs

70%

Percent mentioned wishing their employer(s) had more progressive values

45%

SUMMARY:

Recent graduates are not guaranteed fillers for entry-level roles in election years. The commitment of these young adults to political work begins before a cycle's campaigns are organized *or* announced.

The first-time staffers of 2020 are an example of a micro-generation. Understanding each political cohort's histories gives insight into past and future motivations. Applying this approach across generations can help a diverse range of campaigns improve recruitment and messaging efforts.

Specific candidates and policy stances are especially important to engage young adults. However, many interviewees compromised their more progressive personal beliefs to support Democratic candidates in the 2020 cycle.

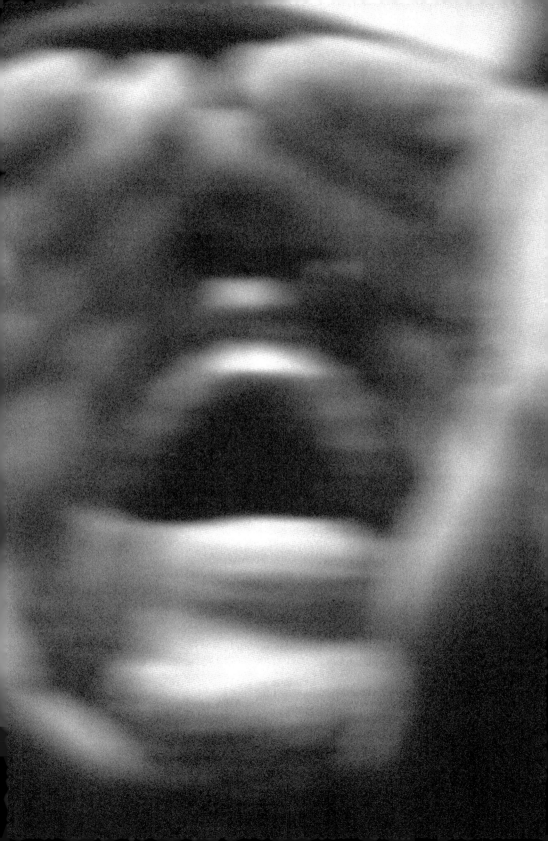

Representation & Inclusion *in* Political Spaces

Inclusive spaces matter to young people. Democratic campaigns and their allies have the opportunity to implement authentic representation as they hire large groups of young employees. This means actively seeking representation from people with a range of backgrounds while avoiding biases; this includes but is not limited to racial, economic groups, educational privilege, geography, sexual orientation, and other underrepresented experiences.

A commitment to creating inclusive workplaces will benefit the Party and movement long-term. Recruiting and supporting a range of staffers who reflect the evolving nature of the Party also allows for more effective engagement with a broader range of constituents.

Women Outnumbered Men as First-Time Staffers

Amongst first-time staffers, approximately 7 out of every 10 staffers were women, with 3.4% of first-time staffers representing genders outside of the binary. Women outnumbered men as first-time staffers despite having less female representation in elected offices.[17] The involvement of these women in Democratic environments is a positive result driven in part by the ongoing efforts of organizations like Emily's List, Emerge America, and others that aim to promote the inclusion of women in political spaces.

Gender Differences in First-Time Staff for Democratic Campaign Work
almost 70% of first time staffers identifying as women in 2020.

Women   Men

Non-binary/gender queer 3.4%

While women made up the majority of entry-level campaign staffers, the strength in numbers did not always yield to positive experiences. Some first-time staffers reported microaggressions and other sexist behavior from their counterparts. Gabbi Perry, a first-time staffer in 2020 on *Alex Morse for Congress* and the *Michigan Democratic Party*, shared her frustration as a woman staffers. Gabbi had repeated instances where her ideas were disregarded, only to be repeated back to her as "new" weeks later. "I remember *countless* moments of being overlooked, shut down, or talked at beyond belief," she recalled. Her experiences were not unique to her— they were also felt by other staffers as well.

Some of the interviewees reported instances of sexual harassment from male volunteers and employees. One staffer recounted being repeatedly called a *'child'* and dealing with inappropriate comments from older male volunteers. She explained she "didn't have the time or energy to do much with these issues."

17. Center for American Women and Politics. (2023). *Gender differences in voter turnout*. Center for American Women and Politics, Eagleton Institute of Politics, Rutgers University-New Brunswick. https://cawp.rutgers.edu/facts/voters/gender-differences-voter-turnout

People in
entry–level
roles often *lack*
the resources
to support
and *protect*
themselves.

Because this volunteer made hundreds of calls a day, this staffer "felt *pressured* to deal with his demeaning behavior so that he would continue to volunteer." Sometimes staffers are in positions where maintaining support of the campaign comes before personal concerns or discomfort.

Many campaigns and cycle-based workplaces are created fast, causing oversights in formal Human Resources departments or processes. It is difficult for staffers, especially those *new* to work environments, to find support to address cases of misconduct or other similar issues.

Working on both *Warren for President* and the *Kansas Democratic Coordinated Campaign* in 2020, an interviewee who wished to remain anonymous, found double standards for her women colleagues. She faced criticism for her own reactions to stress from her role—and was often "teased" and told to *"suck it up"* in consolation. In contrast, outbursts from male colleagues were met with tolerance and support. She also observed that women organizers on her team felt a 'greater responsibility' to complete work to higher standards compared to their male counterparts. Because of this, the women staffers on her team were repeatedly expected to be more productive than their male colleagues. An unfair standard between staffers was created by not having responsibilities for everyone on the team.

In contrast, another female interviewee recalled that men on her team were often placed into general male stereotypes amongst women staffers. She explained the constant rapport of *"This is why I believe in female strong teams"* or *"Guys are the worst except for..."* disregarded her male colleagues, creating *"uncomfortable"* situations for them. Democrats and progressives should address gender discrepancies across workplace culture.

Being disrespected by campaign staff that prided themselves on liberal ideas is a hard truth to face. A nonbinary staffer shared that their gender identity was disregarded by most colleagues on the progressive-facing campaign. Instances of gender inequities and a disconnect in outward messaging verse workplace treatment negatively impacted the experiences of the staffers.

Overall, the high number of women first-time staffers who participated in 2020 is encouraging for the future of the Party and movement. While campaigns operate on a cycle basis, providing safe workspaces and career development (ongoing training, mentorship, and leadership opportunities) is a need for long-term progress in gender representation.

An Absence of BIPOC Representation

Supporting and lifting up people that have a range of experiences and backgrounds within the Party's institutions can better reflect the vision of being an 'party of inclusion.' Despite the Party's growing focus on BIPOC voters, the 2022 midterms saw less support from voters of color than in 2020.[20] Common criticisms that the Party is led by advantaged white-liberals while serving a majority of minority constituents continues to grow.[21] There are some data initiatives within the Party, such as the *Senate Democratic Diversity Initiative,* started in 2007, that challenge diversity quotas. Since the initiative started, numerous Senators have seen an increase in representation among their staff.[22] A commitment to diversity should not only focus on demographic stats—but also work toward understanding non-white, cis-male experiences.

Racial Representation Amongst First-time Staffers in 2020
The majority of first-time staffers identified as white, with a little less than a quarter (23%) representing BIPOC groups.

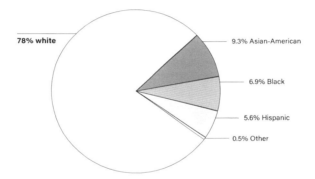

Racial Representation Across Gender
Research found more BIPOC representation among women staffers compared to other genders. This increase aligns with the growing presence of women in entry-level campaign positions.

100% of the nonbinary/genderqueer participants identified as white.

20. Balz, D. (2022, November 3). *Democrats count on huge black turnout, but has the party delivered in return?.* The Washington Post. https://www.washingtonpost.com/politics/interactive/2022/black-vote-elections-2022-democrats

21. Goldberg, Z. (2023, February). *The Rise of College-Educated Democrats.* New York, New York; Manhattan Institute.

22. WP Company. (2022, November 11). *Racial breakdowns for midterms expose shifting electorate.* The Washington Post. https://www.washingtonpost.com/nation/2022/11/11/black-asian-latino-voter-turnout

"We need more leaders that are young and diverse, especially within the realm of politics where we have a significant ability to influence and bring *change.*"

Natalie Valenzuela
One APIA Nevada

The lack of representation can lead to insensitivity and consequential miscommunication between a campaign and BIPOC coalitions. For example, a Georgia-based digital team found and proposed putting up a 'free' mural design in a gentrified neighborhood of Atlanta. The mural, created by a white male artist, featured Black men wearing signs that imitated the historic *'I AM MAN'* signs but with the text *'I AM A VOTE.'* The mural was approved at all levels of the campaign up to senior leadership.

It wasn't until a mid-level BIPOC staffer was cc'd on the email that a concern was brought up. This staffer had to explain to her (primarily white) leadership the negative implications of the mural. The staffer pointed out that if it were to be displayed, it would suggest that the campaign and the Democratic Party views the Black community solely as votes.

The mural did not go up. The situation placed the young female BIPOC staffer in a difficult position where she had to stand up without guaranteed support or any BIPOC leadership to back her up. The fact that the senior staff overlooked the optics of the mural shows how easy it is for campaigns without adequate representation to be out of touch with the communities of color that the Democratic Party relies on for support. Racial representation on campaigns, especially in leadership positions, is important to ensure a range of perspectives or concerns of staffers are heard.

Gabbi Perry observed that the staffers on her campaign did not reflect the district. Despite the Massachusetts district having a large Puerto Rican population, no one on the campaign was fluent in Spanish. Gabbi admitted the U.S. congressional campaign "would have been *exponentially more successful* if we'd had a staff member fluent in Spanish and dedicated to making connections within the Spanish speaking community." The 2020 campaign failed to effectively engage Latinx voters, in part due to a lack of representation among their staff and heavy reliance on non-local advisors.

Other interviewees felt that their campaigns or organizations struggled when it came to BIPOC voter outreach. One digital organizer based in Nevada, explained that many of the voters she had contact with spoke limited or no English. Organizing in Nevada helped this staffer quickly become aware of the need for language accessibility as a standard.

Rachel, a 2020 field organizer based in Kansas, simply stated that the Kansas Democratic Coordinated Campaign "didn't do outreach to minority communities." 'Not having enough time' was the campaign's reasoning for not reaching out to non-white voters. After pushing the campaign and working around certain leadership, Rachel's division of the campaign proudly started a Spanish language phone bank.

Voter contact organizer, Liam Bodlak, saw the difficulties of Democratic messaging connecting with Latinx communities in Miami. He felt that improvements could "take *more than one cycle* of organizing to fully and adequately address them." The common challenges campaigns faced in 2020 with outreach to BIPOC communities advocate for an increase of internal representation in future cycles.

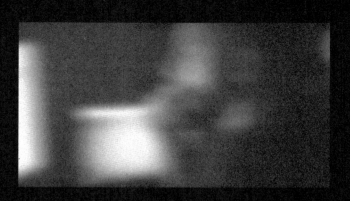

"Diversity is the biggest strength the Democratic Party possesses."

Sonja Thrasher
Tom Steyer 2020 / DCCC / Warnock for Georgia

One person *cannot* represent diversity alone.

Staffers affect the communities that a campaign or organization can have meaningful access to. Building sufficient resources and support for BIPOC staffers is essential for campaigns and organizations to benefit from diverse teams. A single staffer does not represent a diverse workplace. Using staffers solely for access to a particular set of voters is a *'diversity hire,'* rather than an effective way to create racial equity in campaign environments. Having a range of perspectives on a campaign, especially in leadership positions, helps to avoid placing a staffer in uncomfortable or unfair situations.

Similar to the incident involving the Georgia mural, relying on *a sole person* to support a campaign's Latinx outreach (with translations, connections and insight) is *not* truly supporting BIPOC staffers. Ensuring racial representation across all areas and levels of campaign work is important to avoid using people of color solely for access to specific communities.

Jade Ngengi, who worked on *Warren for President* and *Center for Popular Democracy* in the 2020 cycle, pointed out the lack of diverse leadership often leads to the work of BIPOC organizers being undervalued which hurts outreach efforts. She explained that she, "wish[es] the work of BIPOC organizers was *given more than virtue-signaling lip service*. I wish it was valued. I wish the leaders of teams looked like the people who often do the brunt of organizing work." Jade concludes that Democratic and progressive leadership needs to work on better respecting, uplifting, and crediting the work of BIPOC people in the Party.

BIPOC First-Time Staffers were (32%) Less Likely to Secure Consecutive Roles compared to their white counterparts in the 2020 cycle.

% of BIPOC staffers with consecutive political jobs during the cycle

42%

% of white staffers with consecutive political jobs during the cycle

74%

The data collected from this study cannot fully speak to individual groups within BIPOC staffers (e.g. *Black staffers, Latina women, first-generation employees, etc.*). Having less access to specific coalitions of staffers' experiences makes it more challenging to identify and recognize patterns to better support BIPOC staffers.

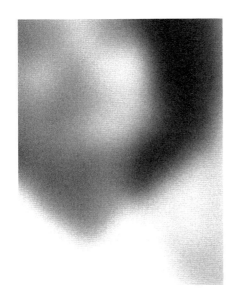

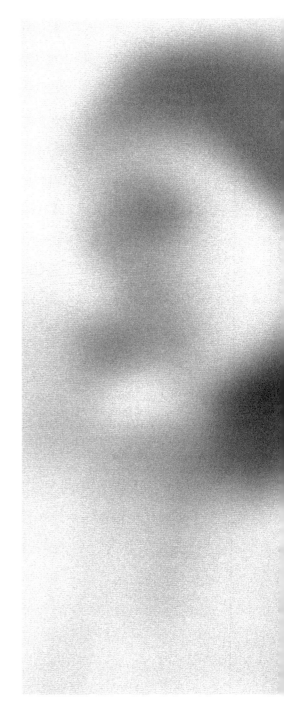

Although it is challenging to pinpoint subsets of BIPOC staffers' realities, overall we found their experiences did differ from those of their white counterparts. First-time BIPOC staffers expressed their struggles with racial tension and discrimination directed toward them—while their white counterparts repeatedly acknowledged their privilege in not experiencing differential treatment. An Iowa caucus organizer, working for both Warren for President and DCCC, observed that BIPOC staffers were "held to a different standard" versus their white counterparts. As one of two Muslims in her entire team, Nelowfar worked through her experiences in Iowa with therapy and support from her BIPOC peers.

Another distinction in the experiences of BIPOC staffers was their lower likelihood of transitioning to multiple roles during the 2020 cycle. Less than half (42%) of BIPOC staffers held more than one paid role, whereas a nearly three-fourths (74%) of first-time, white staffers progressed to a second paid role during the cycle. Individuals who took on consecutive roles during the cycle not only expanded their networks but also gained exposure to promotions, opening future opportunities.

Complexity of BIPOC experiences is lost when only looking at racial representation as a duality (white vs. BIPOC). Future research with *a focus on non-white staff* is needed to create more equitable spaces in the field.

SUMMARY:

Intersectional diversity is important when hiring in campaign and electoral spaces. People who represent a range of backgrounds can create stronger and more effective teams to help guide Party and movement.

While there is an encouraging number of women among first-time campaign staffers in 2020, subtle and *overt* discrimination occurred in the election cycle. The lack of racial representation in campaigns is also clear, with the *majority* of first-time staffers being white staffers.

The focus to promote diversity within campaigns should go beyond gender and race, representing a range of economic classes, sexual orientations and other experiences.

Intentional and *authentic* representation is essential for *future* efforts.

On the Job as *new* staffers.

_The Job: Advantages p.74

_ The Job: Barriers p.80

Nearly every department within a campaign actively seeks to recruit *entry-level* staffers; from digital teams, mobilization efforts, fundraising, finance, and more. The large group of entry-level staffers give a unique workplace experience for recent graduates, in contrast to other industries that may only occasionally hire entry-level roles.

Interviewees credited the benefits of working with their peers, flexibility and strong managers to execute tasks, as well as their opportunity to represent the youngest voting demographic.

While many found advantages to working in the cycle, many encountered *setbacks* in their new roles.

Impostor syndrome, competition, and being overworked were some of the *challenges* faced. Overall, the ability to see their work applied quickly outweighed the negative qualities for most.

The Job:
Advantages

Advantages of
First-Time Staffers

Electoral work offers an opportunity for young adults to work alongside and, be mentored by, some of the best and most experienced individuals in politics. While there is hierarchy and respect in electoral workplaces, everyone at all levels uses the same kitchen to heat late-night dinners.

University of Chicago graduate Megha Bhattacharya worked to get the most out of her first campaign job after graduation. On Warren for President she made a "really conscious effort to connect with as many people as possible." Speaking on the experience of 2020 in February 2021 she reflected, "When you leave college you are leaving this huge network and *losing the sense* of community that you had for the last four years. So many of my friends that went into the private sector or went into consulting had very different experiences because they didn't have access to as many young people." In contrast, campaigns allow staff to be surrounded by a lot of "smart, young, brilliant people who are all working toward the same goal."

Megha continued to explain that, "Campaign jobs give you so much flexibility [for] creating friendships that you don't really find in other jobs. The level of access you have as an entry-level staffer is so valuable." Interviewees valued their roles and recognized the significance of the opportunities they had during the 2020 election cycle. They left with valuable professional experiences and personal relationships that would benefit them in the future.

Liam Bodlak, who worked as a voter contact organizer in Arizona during 2020, found it "*humbling* to work with people who had been organizing since I was in grade school. At first it was an uncomfortable feeling, like I didn't have any 'real world experience' compared to my coworkers, but eventually I was able to learn from them and develop myself as an organizer and person."

Being able to gain a lot of experience and produce work quickly was one of the most valuable parts of working in the 2020 presidential cycle for young staffers interviewed. The fast pace of campaign and electoral organization work allowed first-time staffers to see the outcomes of their work and then adjust efforts for efficiency.

Campaigns that showed trust and collaboration with first-time staffers allowed interviewees to have ownership of the programs and teams they were a part of. As a result, these staffers felt pride in their work.

First-time staffers in 2020 gained valuable insight by holding multiple roles on numerous campaigns and organizations throughout the cycle. Unlike traditional workplaces, where new hires customarily stay at a company for a year or more to maintain relationships, working in the 2020 election cycle provided these individuals with the chance to gain experiences with multiple teams within their first year of work.

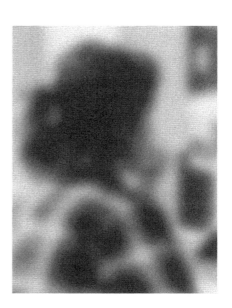

45% had consecutive roles in the cycle.

18%, 3+ jobs
7%, 4+ jobs
.9% 5+ jobs

As campaigns progress beyond the primaries, budgets and teams often expand, giving interviewees opportunities to gain upward professional momentum during a single cycle. Manager and director titles were more likely among first-time staffers who held multiple roles during the cycle. Interviewees found that the cyclical nature of electoral work allows for quicker initial career progression.

A New Jersey organizer reiterated that she felt *"really proud"* that her campaign, *Malinowski for Congress*, worked to "educate phone bankers and voters on a totally new voting system." This organizer felt the active commitment to voter education the campaign had "truly chased every vote." The efforts in 2020 helped Tom Malinowski to win his U.S. Congressional race narrowly.[23] This organizer was able to apply her experiences from the cycle in her role on the virtual Programs team with the Ossoff run-off campaign.

Transferring knowledge across more than one campaign or organization allowed almost half (45%) of first-time staffers to improve their approaches to the work during the single election cycle. Some interviewees held up to 5 different roles during the 2020 cycle. These young adults benefited from knowing how to be more efficient in their teams, better understanding their constituents, avoiding repetitive barriers, and having new opportunities to implement their ideas.

In addition, campaigns that showed trust and collaboration with first-time staffers allowed interviewees to have ownership of the programs and teams they were a part of. As a result, these staffers felt pride in their work.

23. Tom Malinowski lost his seat as New Jersey's 7th Congressional District election in 2022 to the GOP candidate by approx 4.6%.

"My team was very intent on making everyone's voices feel heard and respected. There *wasn't* a huge feeling of hierarchy."

Kiera Manser
Warren for President

"I enjoy the opportunity to surprise people who underestimated me. I moved up *very quickly* during the 2020 cycle. But I also am a white woman, so I think that shapes my experience of being young."

Anonymous

The Job:
Barriers

High-pressure work and a global pandemic are just the start of factors that made the 2020 cycle challenging.

Constant burnout of first-time staffers amplified common barriers that affected their work and aspirations for the 2020 cycle.

Collectively addressing and improving upon staffers' past obstacles creates more unified spaces for future years.

"As a digital staffer, generally the biggest barrier to my success is often how slow the political field can be to adapt to current digital strategy. It can be frustrating feeling like you have to convince people to even try a tactic that the corporate space has proven is effective for years. It can also be hard to feel like you're set up for success when trying a new kind of strategy when you don't receive the resources necessary to make it happen."

Anonymous
Warren for President / Democratic National Convention
Biden Campaign / Inauguration Committee

"I stopped caring about my call numbers after my first few weeks as an organizer. I made *great connections* with the voters I talked to and valued that more than a number on a spreadsheet."

Hannah Gaffney
Organizing Together 2020 / Arizona Legislative District 17 Democrats

Campaign Environment

From the initial announcement to election day, a campaign's goals, internal structures and strategies are constantly moving. The imbalance ends up with unhealthy work environments for some staffers. Starting on day one, many interviewees felt like they were thrown into their first roles without a lot of direction. The rapid nature of campaign organization often results in the absence of internal onboarding processes. First-time staffers, many of whom are recent graduates, felt uncertain on understanding their roles.

While interviewees were open and eager to learn from senior members on the campaign, many of their managers were stretched so thin that they were unable to support entry-level staff. Ezekiel Uriel, a digital content associate for *Jon Ossoff for Senate*, recalled that the digital team was "very understaffed" when he joined which "made proper training very difficult." Ezekiel, starting on the campaign remotely, felt a sense of 'flying blind' because the few senior team members in the department simply "didn't have time to guide me."

Interviewees worked the first few weeks to months trying to figure out how to contribute effectively to their new roles. Rachel, a community team leader and field organizer, remembered that when she started with the *Kansas Democratic Coordinated Campaign* she had to figure out a lot on her own. "We had an onboarding, which gave an overview, but the day-to-day of how to actually do my job was something I struggled with initially."

From an *Arizona* field organizer to becoming the training director for *Jon Ossoff for Senate* one staffer felt that not having "clear direction and concise communication" was one of her biggest *challenges* in the cycle. Inconsistencies in management made it difficult for this first-time staffer to understand her role on the team. "There were days in which I felt micromanaged for silly tasks like sending an email leaving me without time to breathe or think straight. But then there were periods of time in which I was lacking clear instruction/goals—there was never a fully developed plan."

Interviewees repeatedly emphasized that effective leadership and supportive managers helped compensate for the lack of initial direction. Later in the cycle, some of these staffers got to *'pay it back'* as they helped train new staffers.

The fast-track promotion system in electoral settings allows individuals to advance into leadership roles without necessarily strong managerial skills. Professional development being overlooked can easily make or break teams. The oversight impacts the Party long-term, as toxic practices are set as standards and continue upward in leadership. Supporting professional development for staffers outside the context of the election cycle can develop stronger leadership in Party and movement.

In addition to learning the ropes, some first-time staffers struggled to be taken seriously as the youngest members to the campaign. Nelowfar Ahmadi, a field organizer promoted to field manager during the cycle, said that at times she "felt very lost and naive. *I didn't feel like my voice mattered or* that people respected me." Other interviewees also felt that it was hard to contribute to their teams when their opinions and their ideas were not heard or valued. A different staffer on a digital team based in Georgia found being promoted throughout the cycle actually made it more challenging to find her "voice at the table." On her first campaign in the cycle she felt more valued than in her second job. Seniority did not always guarantee a better work environment.

According to interviewees, working in a campaign environment as a first-time staffer sometimes led to relentless peer competition. The toxic culture may have felt particularly intense as many entry-level employees shifted straight from the highly competitive American academic setting to the campaign trail.

An Arizona campaign staffer explained that, "Being a young staffer wasn't where I ran into issues. I felt valued by those who were older or fell into the category of 'senior staffer' more so than I did by my peers." She admitted, "It's a *wacky reality*, but I can't help to think the lack of respect is a result of how competitive campaign staffers are even against one another—it's brutal." It was hard for first-time staffers to tell if leadership was aware of internal competition felt among peers.

Interviewees reported finding themselves continuously striving to outperform both their peers and themselves, pushing beyond their limits. Sometimes campaigns would set goals to break "*arbitrary records*," explained an interviewee. First-time staffers felt that focusing on reaching seemingly random goals encouraged peer competition—while also asking staffers to choose between prioritizing quality verse quantity. Aligning efforts and energy throughout a campaign at all levels will help add transparency and context to support both staffers and the work.

Bad managers can *lose* elections.

Strong leaders can *change* the movement.

The Missing
Focus on Gen Z

Interviewees had difficulty with the lack of Gen Z outreach on campaigns. First-time staff felt that despite the record-breaking 2020 turnout numbers for Gen Z voters, there were missed opportunities to bring young voters to the Democratic movement.[22] In many campaigns, these staffers felt undervalued when their candidates were not addressing or having conversations with young voters. Campaigns and organizations in 2020 were not effective in engaging with Gen Z and Millennials, according to 65% of interviewees.

Interviewees felt connected and saw the value of engaging with younger voters. However, they had to be resourceful while making additional outreach efforts to this demographic. In many cases, first-time staffers felt responsible for including young voters in the messaging of the 2020 cycle.

One North Carolina-based organizer shared that he "wish[ed] we *HAD* gone after younger people, especially in my region where we had four or five colleges and universities. I wish that I had taken on interns and taught students how to organize effectively but again, the campaign did not ever stress the need to bring in college students."

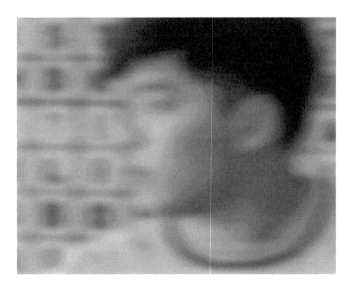

22. Moore, E. (2023, February 6). Gen Z's political power: New Data gives insight into America's youngest voters. NPR. https://www.npr.org/2023/02/06/1154172568/gen-zs-political-power-new-data-gives-insight-into-americas-youngest-voters

A field organizer, who worked with both the *Ed Markey for Senate* and the *Montana Coordinate* campaign, was able to be a part of two different outreach strategies in the same cycle. Based in Boston where there are over fifty colleges and universities in the metropolitan area, the Ed Markey campaign effectively reached out to the youth and used young voters to their advantage. However, Montana's lower population density made it more difficult to target specific demographics of voters, including young people. Young voters had little to no outreach directed at them from the *Montana Coordinate* efforts, according to first-time staffer interviews.

Interviewees found that campaigns relied on areas with a high concentration of young people for their 'youth voter efforts.' Staffers explained that depending on 'easy' targets for youth engagement, Democratic 2020 efforts primarily focused on metropolitan areas versus suburban or rural communities.

Many first-time staffers expressed their *frustration due to the lack* of engagement with young people. Despite raising their concerns, they received minimal or no response. The inclusion of first-time staffers in campaign and electoral spaces played a significant role in compensating strategies that overlooked young voters.

"We failed dramatically in reaching younger voters. We *did not* target them."

Anonymous
Organizing Together NC

COVID-19
Factor

The Transitioning Process

Most campaigns fully migrated to remote work at the beginning of the COVID-19 pandemic in March 2020. This group of first-time staffers, who grew up on digital platforms, found themselves helping their campaigns navigate being socially distanced and working remote. Adjusting to the pandemic had mixed results from interviewees.

Megha Bhattacharya, previously mentioned for her 2020 roles on *Warren for President*, *Democratic National Convention*, *Biden for President*, and *Jon Ossoff for Senate*, explained, "A lot of us who moved [from Warren] to Biden in the last few months of the cycle felt disconnected. Not because of the campaign itself but because we had all been so familiar and comfortable with the physical space of a large HQ office—moving to a completely virtual work setting was a large adjustment."

Transitioning to remote work led staffers like Megha to communicate only with their direct team members. It was harder to have casual conversations and understand how other teams felt when working remotely. There was less room for cross-department collaboration during the early phases of remote campaign work. Reflecting on the effects of COVID-19 on the 2020 staffers, Megha shared that the remote teams were "really siloed" compared to her in-person campaign experience. She reiterated, "As a young person starting their career, campaigns are a great place to find friends and mentorship and keep exploring what you're interested in. The pandemic took a lot of those opportunities to meet new people away from us. There were a lot of efforts to create community through Zoom happy hours and team bonding sessions, but I think most people felt a little isolated."

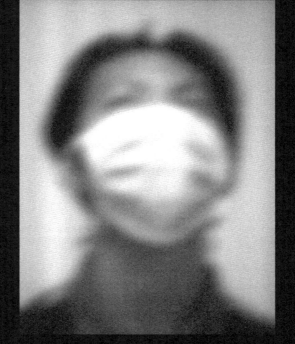

The 2020 general campaigns moved operations almost entirely virtually while most of the country was quarantined at home. A few campaigns, including both of the Georgia Senate Runoff teams, kept a large part of the staff in-person. Heading to Jon Ossoff's Atlanta office was an exciting change for Megha after months of working from home. By the time she joined the Georgia campaign she realized for the most part, "People had gotten used to the fact we were in a pandemic. The [Jon Ossoff] campaign felt so much more like a family because so many of us were in-person—even though there were high health risks." Documenting Ossoff's runoff campaign on the ground in Georgia, within pandemic guidelines, allowed Megha to experience both worlds of the pre-pandemic and pandemic campaign life. For Megha, the Ossoff campaign felt "more like a traditional campaign, even though it wasn't traditional at all."

In contrast, Ezekiel Uriel began working for the *Jon Ossoff for Senate* fully remote while based out of New York. He tried to be "proactive about scheduling casual meetings with people and injecting some personality into regularly scheduled meetings." While he was able to make "some meaningful connections," Ezekiel and other remote staffers felt they "missed out on a lot of the relationships [they] could have formed if this was a normal year."

The Georgia runoff elections benefited from staffers already having systems to navigate remote campaign efforts from the general election. Feeling disconnected pushed staffers to intentionally build (digital) relationships with coworkers. This cohort of staffers had to work harder to seek opportunities on remote campaigns. The advantages of being a young staffer seem to come more naturally with in-person work settings.

Work Flexibility

While the COVID-19 pandemic presented numerous challenges, it also offered some advantages to first-time staffers, particularly in terms of workplace flexibility. First-time staffers looked for opportunities to step up within their roles, leading them to explore new alternative approaches and make valuable contributions to their teams.

Virtual meeting rooms provided a level playing field for first-time staffers, where everyone had equal digital space and presence. The remote platform allowed some first-time staff members to feel more confident and empowered in meeting spaces.

Some first-time staffers found their relationships with organizers and volunteers strengthened during the pandemic. One Pennsylvania based first-time staffer shared, "I was fortunate enough to start on the campaign as an intern pre-pandemic. I honestly think that my relationship with volunteers was stronger during the remote part of the campaign. This may have to do with the fact that I spent more time with volunteers during that time, but I also believe that it was because we were all going through a common struggle. We all looked forward to our time on Zoom calls together in the socially distanced world." Working outside of the central hub of the campaign office helped some first-time staffers connect with younger organizers better while seasoned organizers felt more challenged from having to adjust to digital-first strategies.

First-time staffers, *adaptable* and *dedicated*, embraced and turned out voters despite navigating a global pandemic.

"I have always struggled with anxiety and ADHD, so remaining in a *safe space* filled with strong routines allowed me to feel comfortable and expand my comfort zone without hitting a breaking point."

Anonymous

A 2020 Arizonan first-time staffer reflecting on the election cycle and pandemic shared, "Remote work was one of the best things that could have happened to me. I thrive in spaces which feel routine and safe." The reactive nature of campaigns creates unpredictable work weeks and days. The pandemic helped this Arizona-based staffer build consistency and routine. The staffer also explained they "have always struggled with anxiety and ADHD so being able to remain in a safe space filled with strong routines allowed me to feel comfortable and expand my comfort zone without hitting a breaking point. I have always loved & valued technology. It's not something that scares me."

Similar to an organization's varied approaches to different coalitions or audiences, adopting new strategies to campaign staff and their work environment can increase talent pools and efficiency. Flexible work in election spaces helps create more accessible and equitable employment opportunities for staffers. Reevaluating what roles benefit from remote work can allow flexibility for some staffers. The 2020 presidential and 2022 midterm cycles show campaigns and progressive organizations can be successful while offering remote or hybrid work opportunities.

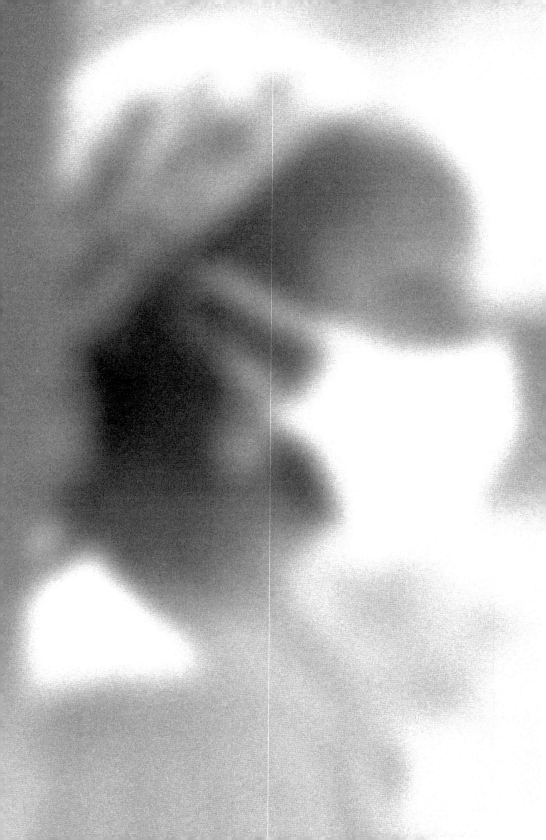

A Reminder of the Impact of Connections

The COVID-19 pandemic was a reminder that campaigns and the election season are opportunities to build multi-generational connections across regions. Hannah Gaffney, a 2020 first-time organizer with *Arizona Legislative District 17 Democrats,* shared, "With COVID-19 and being in a district with an older population, a lot of voters were lonely and just wanted to talk with someone. One man I talked with at the beginning of COVID-19 told me that his wife had recently passed away. He lived alone and had no human interaction for days until I called him. Richard called me *once a week* for the next 6 months to see how the campaign was doing and what I was up to in life. Making these types of connections with voters was much more impactful and allowed them to remember me, my campaign, and the candidates better because they actually felt like someone cared about them beyond their political preferences; and that was crucial in gaining the support of a lot of people who were on the fence."

Having meaningful connections is important for voters of all ages. A Michigan-based organizer who primarily supported youth voters during the cycle, learned her job was more than simply "getting out to vote but taking the time to have mean-ingful conversations on voter info and how voting can *impact* one's life in the *short* and *long term*."

The challenge of quickly adapting to COVID-19 made the impact of building connections between campaigns and voters more difficult. However, people were more open to discussing their feelings of isolation and wanting connections.

To interviewees, non-metropolitan districts felt really spread apart during the pandemic. Ellen Smith was proud of the relational organizing training program she helped create with a coordinate campaign. She did speculate that "showing up [in-person] could have actually made a difference" with her campaign's efforts in Montana. While campaigns and organiza-tions found additional ways to connect with voters, replacing the connections of being on the ground was hard.

A Pandemic of Burnout

Burnout was (and is expected to continue to be) the most common experience across all levels of campaign work, from local elections to national races, impacting experiences and performance of first-time staffers. Burnout can have both physical and emotional consequences that can worsen over time if not addressed. Common signs of burnout are decreases in overall physical and mental health, as well as emotional symptoms such as feelings of failure and self-doubt, becoming overly cynical, and disassociating from work and personal life.

Burnout is almost unavoidable due to the intense and relatively short nature of election work. Knowing that the election cycle won't last forever, staffers at all levels often feel a sense of urgency to push themselves harder. This mindset leads to overworking and neglecting self-care, both of which are common causes of burnout in campaign-based work. First-time campaign staffers were likely to push themselves and work under immense pressure. Retaining institutional knowledge in campaign work partly depends on keeping staffers in the industry. Decreasing burnout in campaign environments will make working in the field long-term more sustainable.

We found that 90% of first-time staffers experienced burnout without proper support and resources in the 2020 election cycle. The consequences of guaranteed burnout, particularly among young staffers, needs to be addressed in order to prevent long-term physical and mental health problems in the Party. In turn, the Party and movement will better preserve the talent and experiences of electoral staffers to leverage in future campaign cycles.

To analyze burnout amongst interviewees, we divided the responses into two phases: 'During the Cycle' and 'Ending and Post-Cycle.' Considering the impact of burnout during both of these phases to develop improved work environments for staffers.

Campaigns compromise mental health.

90% experience burnout.

During the Cycle

Entry-level staffers had less experience navigating the workplace and political environments. Generally, they lacked comparisons of healthy workplace standards and boundaries, which made it difficult for them to establish clear boundaries to protect themselves from burnout.

First-time campaign staffers faced multiple challenges as they juggled completing final semesters of school, caring for family members, managing their mental health, and adapting to new surroundings in some cases. Many did not feel their responsibilities, both within and outside of work, were acknowledged or appropriately considered.

9 out of 10 first-time staffers experienced burnout due to their roles in the election cycle. For the most part, campaigns, and organizations did not prioritize preventing burnout and promoting the mental well-being of their staff in 2020. The staffers who did not experience burnout felt supported by their managers. Managerial support, such as regular check-ins and workload monitoring, can help prevent burnout, especially for those less experienced in coping with political work and stress.

Sonja Thrasher quickly learned that "there are no real hours on campaigns." She described developing, 'campaign brain' where she found herself routinely "replying to emails at midnight" while working as an organizer for *Tom Steyer 2020*, the *DCCC*, and *Warnock for Georgia* in 2020. Sonja along with other interviewees made clear that "work-life balance is virtually non-existent" as a campaign staffer. Interviewees knew they shouldn't have put so much pressure on themselves however, "when doing what you feel is such important work, it is hard not to throw yourself into it completely," explained Sonja. While understaffed teams are often so due to budget and financial limitations, they felt an obligation to step-in as the campaign or organization needed.

A lot of the programs that the entry-level staffers were a part of had very limited resources. This impacted the overall effectiveness and efficiency of a campaign or organization's operations and the staffers on a personal level. Kiera Manser, fundraising producer *Warren for President* commented, "The biggest hurdle for me was being stretched so thin."

Another organizer based in Michigan recognized that their team wasn't given enough resources to effectively reach out to young voters. Her state-focused team "had to be creative" if they wanted to support the younger demographic of voters. The campaign "scraped together and created a voter universe from the ground up using our own Instagram [direct messages]."

From state run efforts to national platforms, Kiera also noted Warren for President's organizing program wasn't as "robust as it should be." There were inefficiencies to the programs she worked on directly because of understaffing. The ambitious goals of the campaign often trickle down to weigh individual staffers in overwhelming numbers of quotas and workloads.

"I don't really feel like anyone didn't experience burnout."

Anonymous
Amy McGrath for Senate

Insufficient support of campaign efforts doesn't just affect staffers, but also volunteers. Elliot Richardson, a campus organizer for the city of Boston, found that insufficient support particularly affected efforts to engage with voters who typically have less resources. It was complicated for the campaign to ask people to support the campaign when they didn't "have the resources to get involved or canvas." Elliot felt it was difficult seeing student volunteers who "often didn't have their own cars and couldn't afford merch as many other volunteers could."

Hannah Gaffney also had similar feelings, admitting that she wished she could have delegated more to her interns but she felt guilty because she "didn't want to overload them with responsibilities from an unpaid internship that they balanced with school and extracurriculars."

Another interviewee shared that it was difficult to see unpaid fellowships next to, "*record breaking* fundraising numbers," but understaffed teams and "no investments in areas like paying working class young voters." It is not practical to rely on unpaid work from young people. Campaign culture that lacks resources to support their staff and volunteers lead to burnout for all, regardless type or level of election.

Burnout tended to intensify toward the end of the election cycle, primarily due to factors such as working seven days a week with increased workloads associated with final GOTV (Get Out the Vote) and election day efforts. Campaign and electoral organization leadership should prepare for increased rates of burnout as the campaigns progress by implementing additional strategies to provide resources and actionable support for staffers. Addressing burnout early on and having systems in place to prepare staffers approaching election day can help mitigate the long-term physical and mental health consequences that almost all first-time staffers experienced in 2020.

The post-election transition out of campaign work can be challenging. Win or lose, interviewees expressed it was difficult mentally to navigate the end of a cycle for the first time. Once all-hands meetings have concluded and campaign Slack channels are archived, staffers are reminded of the finite nature of the infrastructures of campaigns and cycle-focused organizations. A lot of first-time campaign staffers reported experiencing burnout starting after the campaign had ended as they dealt with the loss of the 24/7 community from co-workers and volunteers. The ending of the election cycle is a sudden change of pace for staffers.

"It's *unfair* to ask young campaign staffers to set these boundaries because they may hurt their future networking chances if they do not jump when they're asked to."

Anonymous

An Arizona-based staffer explained in early 2021, a few months after the 2020 efforts had concluded, that, "it's hard to know what to do next. It's hard to feel like you were running a marathon nonstop and then *boom*, everything ends. Your friendships, routines, the chaos—it's a really weird feeling. It felt like it ended so suddenly—we had an end date, we knew when Election Day was, but I wasn't mentally prepared for how friendships would fade and how losing a race could make you feel tiny and like you sacrificed a TON for nothing."

Campaigns going radio silent after the end of the cycle leaves staffers disconnected and uncertain about their next steps. Planning for and preparing staff for the end of a campaign cycle is often overlooked and not a responsibility of campaigns or the Party.

How a candidates' campaign wraps up has a lasting impact on staffers. Not having available or helpful resources for burnout bring some to the conclusion that the system they worked for doesn't value individuals.

Long-term physical and mental health problems from working in electoral spaces are avoidable. Campaigns and the Party can use the post-cycle period to unify staffers and set them paths for those interested to continue supporting the Party's values in off-election years. Having a plan to combat burnout early on better supports staffers during and after the cycle.

Imperfect Solutions;
Advice & Unionizing

First-time staffers found their own methods of protecting themselves from election cycle burnout. Many staffers emphasized setting boundaries so they would not be pushed past their limits. A staffer on the *Warren for President* campaign recommends to, "make your boundaries known as early as possible. When I first started my full-time position I told my manager that I would need time off every week for therapy and church. We were able to agree on clear expectations and boundaries because I made my needs known at the beginning of our work together." Setting up boundaries before the campaign intensifies can help avoid extreme burnout.

It was also important for first-time staffers to have a life outside of politics and work. This might include checking in with friends and family outside of work, as well as taking time for yourself. An LA-based first-time staffer recalled, "for me, taking 20-30 minutes to eat breakfast, lunch, or dinner without working was really important to stay sane." Setting up time boundaries with work helped staffers manage their experiences of burnout. In addition, guaranteed time off and sufficient sleep were important to staffers preventing burnout. During busy periods, causal communication between peers can fade away. Having check-ins with fellow co-workers helped them to feel they were not alone and was a coping method against burnout.

Setting realistic expectations by managers and campaign leadership helped to manage burnout. Having transparency around what would be the day(s) off during the week helps staffers to plan their time and rest outside of work hours. Establishing periods for being officially offline also helped relieve pressure of availability experienced by interviewees.

"Unionize and develop relationships with union leadership before *crisis* hits."

Jace Ritchey
Warren for President

The need for unionization was brought up by first-time staffers repeatedly when speaking on their experiences of burning out. The systemic combination of long hours, tight deadlines, minimal job security, and lack of overtime pay is larger than the single conversations or incidents recounted by interviewees. Unions provide staffers with the power to collectively negotiate for better wages, benefits, and working conditions. By unionizing, staffers can ensure that they are fairly compensated for their work and have access to resources post-campaign.

In response to problematic trends in campaign work and environments, Bernie 2020 became the first presidential campaign to unionize.[25] Several other Democratic campaigns followed suit to also unionize in 2020. Presidential campaigns including those of Corey Booker, Pete Buttigieg, Julian Castro, Bernie Sanders and Elizabeth Warren unionized. In addition, Rep. Alexandria Ocasio-Cortez (D-N.Y.), Joe Kennedy III (Mass.), Sen. Ed Markey (Mass.), and Mike Siegel in Texas's 10th District unionized in 2020. The unionization of campaigns made it to a few Democratic House races too; Rep. Deb Haaland (D-N.Mex.), Max Rose (D-N.Y.), and Pramila Jayapal (D-Wash.) also unionized.[26]

Bernie Sanders' 2020 presidential campaign contract helped staffers working eight hours or more have two 15-minute breaks and a 30-minute paid lunch period while Warren's 2020 union contract advocated for 60-hour workweeks.[27] *AP News* reported that staffers on Sanders' 2020 campaign, "working 16 consecutive hours would get a 12-hour rest period before starting again. It also gave staffers the right to request time off *'blackout days'* of up to three days in a row, though such requests were limited as big elections approached."[28]

25. Griffiths, B. D. (2019, March 15). *Bernie Sanders' staffers unionize in first for presidential campaign.* Politico. https://www.politico.com/story/2019/03/15/bernie-campaign-2020-staff-union-1223914

26. Desai, S. (2019, August 24). *Why 2020 campaign workers are suddenly unionizing.* The Atlantic. https://www.theatlantic.com/politics/archive/2019/08/2020-campaigns-unionize-sanders-warren-booker-castro/596599

27. Axelrod, T. (2019, September 28). *Warren's campaign reaches tentative deal to unionize.* The Hill. https://thehill.com/homenews/campaign/463508-warren-campaign-reaches-tentative-union-deal

28. Weissert, W. (2023, March 23). *Pro-labor? Biden aims to prove it with unionized 2024 staff.* AP NEWS. https://apnews.com/article/biden-campaign-2024-union-labor-254d11b044a4bf2209e-c434a702a1b96

Previously mentioned field organizer, Hannah Gaffney, recommended, if possible, for staff to "unionize early and set really strict standards for the workplace." In 2020, Hannah supported Democrats in Arizona's Legislative District 17. She observed that despite being unionized, staffers would still need to advocate for work-life balance and assert their needs. Hannah explained that, "the campaign will start to push back [against the union contracts] and 'give you opportunities' to work more hours than your union contract states, which is a great way to earn more money, but don't allow it to become an expectation."

Although staff unionization in campaigns is increasingly common, it is not yet the norm among Democratic and progressive organizations. As Joe Biden emerged as the front-runner and Democratic nominee in 2020, staffers from other unionized campaigns began joining their general election efforts. Staff helped the campaign unionize in May 2020, about a year after *Biden for President* started.

The Biden re-election campaign proactively initiated union negotiations before the 2024 campaign was officially announced in April 2023.[23] While the campaign started unionizing earlier than the prior cycle, the Biden campaign had not started staffing up at the time of the first negotiations. This left many staffers, including entry-level organizers, out of initial conversations.

Despite progress in union involvement, the benefits sometimes felt more theoretical than actionable. When speaking to first-time staffers, it became clear that while unions helped to improve campaign standards, it did not always lead to sufficient day-to-day changes. The rate of burnout in electoral work is avoidable. Prioritizing the well-being of the electoral staffers adds stability in the Democratic Party and progressive movement.

SUMMARY:

For politically engaged young people looking to kick-start their careers, the 2020 campaign provided a valuable opportunity to gain quick and unique experiences, which brought both long-term benefits and challenges.

Overall, most first-time staffers had positive experiences, with 77.5% of our interviewees interested in remaining in the field in some capacity. The critiques of these staffers provide a learning opportunity for *future* campaigns and organizations to emphasize alternative approaches to better *support* staffers.

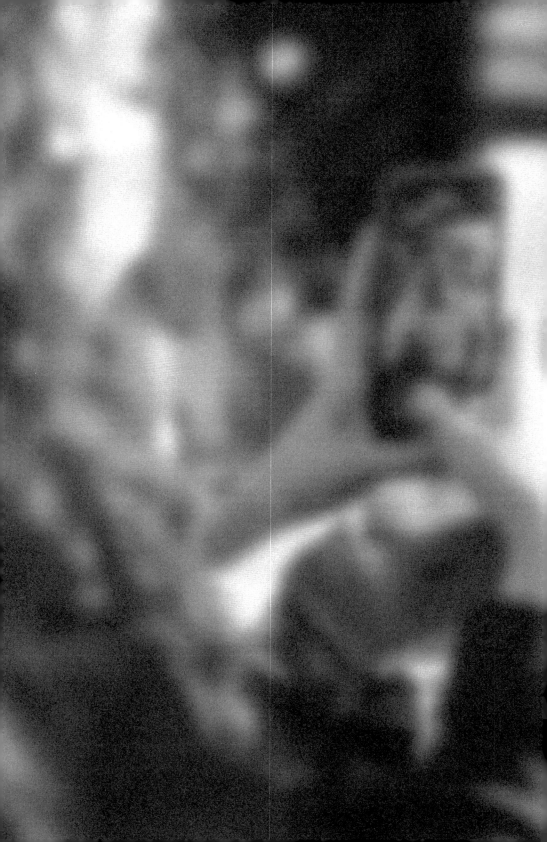

Conclusion

More transparency, long-term
strategies, and equity is needed
in campaign spaces.

Inheriting knowledge in cyclical Democratic & *progressive* spaces will create more efficient and sustainable systems.

Supporting sharing insights across electoral work at all levels will help improve the current systems.

The interviewees of *One Year in Politics* grew from the privileges of inheriting knowledge throughout the 2020 cycle.

Taking time to look at the experiences and composition of campaigns can support both *individual* staffers and the *overall* movement. For instance, being aware that entry-level roles were predominantly filled by women in 2020 can bring a continued commitment to support this group as they advance into higher positions that have historically had less gender diversity. *Or* by having access to reporting on the stories of BIPOC first-time staffers can provide insight into future challenges and strengths for the Party and movement. This, in turn, can help focus on creating safer workplace environments that advocate for more racial diversity.

Young people are important in shaping the future of the Democratic Party and the progressive movement. These interviewees will likely continue to impact the future of the Party, with nearly 8 out of every 10 interviewees interested in remaining in the field.

Their involvement in the 2020 election cycle also underscores the need for diverse representation on campaigns—as the first-time staffers actively subsidized outreach to their peers and young adult voters.

Many of the experiences from interviewees were not single instances but common trends. Promoting transparency between campaigns and staffers' insights allows staffers to identify patterns, creating more opportunities for people to advocate themselves and better work.

Unionizing campaigns in 2020 provided further support; however, many staffers sought out additional resources to cope with the workplace and high burnout rates.

For electoral work to improve, the Party must recognize the complexity of challenges. Solutions will be more than a single effort, but accountability is necessary.

Committing to retaining and exchanging knowledge will support sustainability within the temporary campaign and electoral structures.

The
Interviews

_Responses are listed anonymously to speak as a unit.

Question 1

What or who led you to being involved in the 2020 election cycle?

"I grew up in DC and had always been surrounded by politics. I resisted the idea that I would work in campaigns until after the 2016 election. It was enough of a wake-up call that I decided I wanted to pursue politics. I interned for Senator Kamala Harris and Senator Kirsten Gillibrand on Capitol Hill in the summer of 2018, and did some volunteering through Swing Left.

My internship led me to decide I wanted to work for now-VP Harris if/when she announced she was running, and my experience knocking doors for House candidates in VA made me want to be an organizer. I graduated college in May 2019 and a month later, packed up and moved to Iowa to be an organizer for her." ⁘

"In June 2019, I felt like I wasn't doing enough during what was shaping up to be a contentious election. Knowing that Joe Biden was the presumptive nominee, I just happened to come across the candidate on Facebook, felt good about him, and asked [the campaign] how I could help." ⁘

"Desiree Tims, Democratic candidate for U.S. House Ohio District 10, led me to work in this cycle. I liked her message and wanted her experience and expertise to replace the opponent." ⁘

"I became interested in politics during the 2018 midterm cycle. As a result, in 2020, I joined Jaime Harrison for U.S. Senate as a full-time digital associate while volunteering for Pete Buttigieg's campaign on an organizing level-the cultural and ethnic politics of the area are so deeply set that it'll take more than one cycle of organizing to fully and adequately address them." ⁘

"On Election Night in 2016, my dad called me crying and said he felt like he was back in Apartheid-era South Africa (where he's from). That struck a chord with me, and I remember thinking, "Okay, when I graduate in 2020, Trump's first term will be up— I have to be a part of that." ⁂

"I graduated with a degree in Political Sciences during COVID. Jobs were hard to come by. My goal was (and is) to work on a legislative team, but after talking to people in the field, I eventually realized that my best chance at getting a job would be to work with a campaign. I interviewed at a few places and liked the vibe I got from the organization I eventually worked for." ⁂

"I have always had the drive to make the world a better place so when the opportunity came to get involved, first as an intern on a presidential [campaign] and then as an organizer on a coordinated [campaign], I jumped at the chance." ⁂

"I was on the executive board of my campus's College Dems group and made connections with the state party. I later worked as a fellow on a Senate campaign and was recruited to work as a Field Organizer for the coordinated campaign." ⁂

"I was unemployed, just out of grad school, and wanted to do something productive. I fell in love with Senator Warren, and things snowballed from there." ⁂

"I was terrified of another four years of Donald Trump. I turned down multiple full-time job offers to work on a campaign [that] resonated with me." ⁂

"Opportunity, circumstance, and wanting to get Jim Jordan out of office led me to participate in the 2020 election cycle. I was supposed to graduate in August 2020, travel to Indonesia and become a professional SCUBA diver. COVID threw a wrench in these plans.

I had seen Elizabeth Warren on Twitter before, and I decided to sign up to be a volunteer. I hadn't heard anything back in two weeks, so I decided to tweet at her, and almost immediately, someone from the campaign reached out to me.

I volunteered on my first phonebank the next day, and shortly after that, I interviewed to become an intern. After the field organizer, who was my manager, stepped away, I interviewed for the position and became a paid member of the team." ⁂

"By graduating in 2019, I would be graduating in the most important election of my lifetime. Working on the 2020 election felt like the most important thing I could do out of undergrad, and I still think that way. So many young people became engaged politically due to the results of the 2016 election, and if we didn't have such increased youth engagement in 2020, I don't know if things would have turned out the way they did. I was passionate and sure that I needed to be involved in the 2020 cycle, and when I saw a friend had started working on a campaign I was interested in, I immediately applied. The rest is actual history!" ⁂

Q1 / *What or who led you to being involved in the 2020 election cycle?*

"I thought Elizabeth Warren was the presidential candidate with the best shot of utilizing the levers of power to implement climate justice policies and make Big Structural Change. I could think of nothing more important than fighting for that future and a candidate that I thought could sell those structural changes to the rest of the party." ⁂

"Organizing Corps. With the step down of Isakson, Georgia would have two senate seats open and I knew that we would be the battleground to look out for, and flipping state leg seats so the Democrats could control redistricting." ⁂

"I interned at the ACLU in D.C. in the 2018 midterms as an undergrad. I ended up working on Peer to Peer (P2P). When I graduated in 2019, I was looking for a job in progressive non-profits and applied to do P2P for *Warren for President*." ⁂

"My role as a macro social worker led me to be involved in the 2020 cycle." ⁂

"I graduated from college in December 2018 and had no idea what I wanted to do. After bussing tables for a few months, a college advisor helped me set up a meeting with someone who runs a firm that supports campaigns in the Columbus area. She told me campaigns are a great place to start to get into politics and government work and encouraged me to get in touch with one of the presidential teams in Iowa or New Hampshire. A few applications later and I was moving to Iowa at the end of August to work on Joe Biden's campaign as a Field Organizer." ⁂

"January to May 2020 was the end of my senior year at Indiana University. This time coincided with the campaign heating up into its final push. Having studied Journalism and Political Science, I was keenly aware of what was going on in the news day to day and how the candidates were positioning themselves in the race.

Given my fascination with American history, I knew I was interested in getting involved with politics as I was in the heat of my initial job search, but I didn't really know how to get involved. While writing a final for one of my courses comparing Trump's weak federal response to the COVID-19 pandemic with Herbert Hoover's lack of action in response to the growing financial crisis in the late 1920s, it was impossible to ignore the themes of history echoing into today's political consciousness. As a young Jewish American, Trump's "America First" rhetoric harkened back to the campaign of Charles Lindbergh, whose anti-globalist, antisemitic rhetoric nearly won out in the early 1930s. As a student of history, I realized that our democracy is something that we have to constantly work for, and I found" a job in the Biden campaign." ⁂

"I couldn't find a job after graduating in May 2020. I contacted an organizer on LinkedIn to network, and she sent me the name of the Progressive Turnout Project. I applied and honestly had no idea what to expect." ⁂

"I graduated from college in May 2020. I was unsure whether my long-term future was in politics, but I felt that the stakes of the 2020 election were far too high to sit it out."

Q1 / *What or who led you to being involved in the 2020 election cycle?*

"I knew *to bring change*, I would have to *put in the work*. I wanted to get my first experience working with a political organization. My role as a digital organizer in the 2020 campaign cycle allowed me to work for a candidate that reflected some of my interests and advocated for the Asian American Pacific Islander community in my state. I wanted to make sure I did everything I was able to mobilize my community to vote while advocating for progressive issues and make sure people's voices were heard." ⁂

"I was preparing to graduate from college in June 2019 and looking for a job or internship. I switched majors the semester after Trump took office from engineering to public policy and wanted to get into the fight to unseat him. I didn't want to regret not doing what I could to get out the most corrupt president in history OUT. I identified as a Progressive and liked Elizabeth's messaging: I loved how aggressive she was on big banks, and her transition from academia to policy resonated with me.

I applied to the campaign without connections or understanding what it meant to be an organizer. I had volunteered at local races and did student advocacy but nothing else. I wanted to understand the electorate better, have meaningful but difficult conversations, and educate people on these important and revolutionary policy ideas." ⁂

"Elizabeth Warren! My first job was on a congressional race, but I got a field fellowship with *Iowa for Warren*, which got me into the field." ⁂

"Going into 2020 I knew I wanted to work for a woman. I felt like it was time, and from the women that I saw entering the race I felt more than excited about many of them.— I thought like yeah that's an easy criteria to start thinking about. I just kind of watched the race unfold a little bit.

I got rejected from several jobs before I got one. I went through the interview process a couple of times and kept getting rejected and kept aggressively following up with everyone on the campaign I had spoken to. About every week I would be like 'Hello, are there any more jobs? Did you know I can kind of do this other thing? —because I really, really wanted to work for her.'

It was applying to open jobs. It was also going to campaign events where I was at school and volunteering as much as I could. I talked to the staff members I met at those opportunities and say that I was trying to work for the campaign and if they could put in a good word with everyone I could. I was regularly reaching out to people that were on the campaign." ⁂

"I had been waiting for the 2020 elections for years. Not only was our chance to get rid of Donald Trump, but it was also *a chance to build progressive power* and elect people who would work to fight the crises we're facing at the scales which they demand. As a young person, I feel the weight of the climate crisis and the urgency with which we must act. In the fall of 2019, my sophomore year, I made the decision to take a year off from school and worked on two campaigns for the next ten months. The 2020 elections signified a turning point and a decisive moment in history, and I knew I wanted to be part of it." ⁂

"I had been involved in the political world through internships and volunteering for a few years before the cycle began, but I was unsure of who my first choice was in the Democratic 2020 primary for president until about June 2019. When I heard Elizabeth Warren speak, I could see the vision she had for this country and knew she had the ~plans~ to back it up. I felt like the energy around her was contagious, and I had to do everything I could to work on her campaign." ⁂

"As a young student with a disability and an assault survivor who's always been represented by Republicans in my district, I got involved in the 2020 campaign cycle because my vision for radical compassion depended on this election.

I knocked on thousands of doors as a high school junior in 2019 for a successful local race. In 2020, I began organizing by creating a program to plug around 150 high school and college students into under-funded and understaffed state legislature races. I knew so many people who didn't know where to start, and I took it upon myself to help them get into organizing in ways that were non-exploitative and community-based. The stakes were so high that I couldn't just step back." ⁂

"...a chance to build *progressive power* and elect people who would work to fight the crises we're facing at the scales which they demand."

"Growing up, as soon as I learned my high school graduation year (2016) was the year of a presidential election, I was ecstatic. I knew that meant that four years later, when I would wrap up my undergraduate degree, it would be another presidential election. It felt like perfect timing.

What I didn't know, of course, was that Donald Trump would be elected, the horrors we would face as a result of his presidency, nor the COVID-19 pandemic, which would put a pause on any and all sense of normalcy. So while I had always hoped to be involved in the 2020 election cycle, I didn't know how or if it was something that would become a reality. ⁂

In November of 2019, after being rejected from an internship with the Arizona State Legislature (a blessing in disguise), my dad received a text message meant for me from the Organizing Corps. Of course, my curious father played along, received the details for the application, and shortly after texted me about the opportunity. At first, I thought it was a scam; it all seemed like it was too good to be true. But as it turns out, it wasn't a scam. It was perfect timing and my "in" to the 2020 election cycle."⁂

"I fell in love with campaign life during the 2018 cycle [in] my final semester of college. I wasn't sure if I was going to work on a campaign, but the advice I got from everyone while graduating was to work on a presidential campaign if I could, and they were very right!

I was already really interested in Warren, and she seemed more and more like the best candidate to me. Also, one of my best friends from college was working on her 2018 senate campaign. I applied for a job at Warren the day she announced she might run, and seven months later they finally contacted me." ⁂

Question 2

What's your take on being one of
the youngest staffers in the room?

"We were so committed, we were expected to be on the clock 24/7." ∴

"It was weird, but expected. I was lucky enough to be on a team where I felt my input was valued despite being so new, but that may have been because my Field Director was a year or two older than I was." ∴

"Most of the staffers were on the younger side, so it was generally fine and the campaign was really banking on young voters turning out to the polls to win, so I felt like our perspective was listened to and valued." ∴

"To be honest, I felt very lost and naive. I didn't feel like my voice mattered or that people respected me. Mind you, most of that comes from being a woman of color from a poor background in a space that's mostly white and upper-middle class. That's a different conversation that I'm happy to have." ∴

"I really enjoyed it. I felt proud to be working alongside more seasoned staffers and there was so much to learn from them. My experience was also completely positive. All the more experienced staffers I worked with and became friends with were friendly, kind, and supportive. I never felt that my being younger was a hindrance in the campaign environment (although I always liked it when someone mistook me for being older!) It also bonds you with the other young staffers." ∴

"My team was really young. I think this cycle, the rooms themselves were younger, which is so exciting! Especially with COVID, a lot of folks took time off school or were taking gap years to be a part of the campaign." ∴

"I think it's important; we need more leaders that are young and diverse, especially within the realm of politics where we have a significant ability to influence and bring change." ∴

"I was a campus organizer. I mainly worked with folks slightly younger than me. That was incredibly rewarding in many ways; I got to be my genuine self and talk the way I do to my peers and make friends in ways that many of my coworkers with older volunteers could not. Most of the other staffers on my team were about my age. I never felt out of place." ⁂

"It was odd. I knew most people were in their 20's and 30's so I didn't feel that off until I started having conversations with coworkers. They would talk about previous campaign cycles they'd been part of and seemed so much more experienced than I was. No one ever purposefully made me feel inadequate, but I was often aware that I was one of three people in HQ born in the late '90s.

On the other hand, everyone I met was so enthusiastic about their work and excited that I wanted to be part of the movement. Everyone was willing to give advice and offered help when the campaign ended. It was a very supportive environment." ⁂

"Everyone on the organizing team seemed to be between the ages of 20-28, so I really didn't feel young. Actually, at times, I felt old. My boss was significantly younger than I was and had years of experience on me. I wish I'd been introduced to organizing at a younger age." ⁂

"I didn't mind [being the youngest staffer]— I enjoy the opportunity to surprise people who underestimated me. I moved up very quickly during the 2020 cycle. But I also am a white woman, so I think that shapes my experience of being young." ⁂

"I remember the first week of work being overwhelmed by how hard and how much everyone worked. I stayed 'online' on Slack until 10 PM, working on various small tasks to 'prove my worth' on my team. Most of the time, my opinions and suggestions were valued in my entry-level position. However, as I progressed upward throughout the 2020 cycle, having a voice at the table became more challenging. It wasn't easy to fully embrace my mid-level position in the second campaign. It helped give me insight into some of the hoops leadership faces." ⁂

"Surprisingly, I wasn't the youngest in the room, my manager was younger than me. Most people on the campaign were under 35 so no one seemed that much older than me. Also, everyone was extremely respectful and kind to everyone else, regardless of age. My team was very intent on making everyone's voices feel heard and respected. There wasn't a huge feeling of hierarchy, again just on my team. At my new job after the campaign however...age is a different story." ⁂

"I was not the youngest staffer, someone else in my region was actually still in college and taking classes during the Fall 2020 semester which I thought was wild because who has the time to work a 60-hour work week and take classes on top of that. I liked my region in North Carolina because we were so spread out in ages and backgrounds. A lot of the people I worked with were not full-time political staffers, they just joined the campaign because they believed in putting Democrats back in the White House/Senate/House of Representatives." ⁂

Q2 / *What's your take on being one of the youngest staffers in the room?*

"Growing up, as soon as I learned my high school graduation year (2016) was the year of a presidential election, I was ecstatic. I knew that meant that four years later, when I would wrap up my undergraduate degree, it would be another presidential election. 2020 felt like perfect timing.

What I didn't know, of course, was that Donald Trump would be elected, the horrors we would face as a result of his presidency, nor the COVID-19 pandemic, which would put a pause on any and all sense of normalcy. So while I had always *hoped* to be involved in the 2020 election cycle, I didn't know how or if it was something that would become a reality.

In November of 2019, after being rejected from an internship with the Arizona State Legislature (a blessing in disguise), my dad received a text message meant for me from the *Organizing Corps*. Of course, my curious father played along, received the details for the application, and shortly after texted me about the opportunity. At first, I thought it was a scam; it all seemed like it was too good to be true. But as it turns out, it wasn't a scam. It was *perfect timing* and my "in" to the 2020 election cycle." ⁂

"I graduated from college in December 2018 and had no idea what I wanted to do. After bussing tables for a few months, a college advisor helped me set up a meeting with someone who runs a firm that supports campaigns in the Columbus area. She told me campaigns are a great place to start to get into politics and government work and encouraged me to get in touch with one of the presidential teams in Iowa or New Hampshire. A few applications later and I was moving to Iowa at the end of August to work on Joe Biden's campaign as a Field Organizer." ⁂

"On the Pennsylvania coordinated campaign, most of the staffers were all young, twenty-somethings looking to make a difference. Given that we were all young, romantic, and full of energy, it was a great environment to be working an abundant number of hours. As evident by the social movements of the past several years, our generation takes a different perspective on politics and the world then those before us. It felt important to be a part of the team communicating the campaign's message." ⁂

"My boss was also 22, so it never seemed quite so daunting." ⁂

"I was more afraid of being *less experienced* than I [was] from being young. Others my age/year in school had done far more than me in the world of campaigns. I almost constantly felt intimidated.

Truthfully, I was afraid of seeming dumb or behind. Being a young staffer wasn't where I ran into issues. I felt valued by those who were older or fell into the category of 'senior staffer' more so than I did by my peers. It's a wacky reality, but I can't help to think it's a result of how competitive campaign staffers are even against one another— it's brutal." ⁂

"This work can either turn you into a really awful careerist or push you to become a better person in your work. Too many people became the former, and I desperately want to be grouped in with the latter someday." ⁂

"I was more afraid of being less experienced *than* I was from being young."

"It was really difficult. I worked on a local campaign in Arizona that had their ideas of what campaigning and canvassing should be. A lot of these approaches weren't feasible due to the pandemic. I tried to bring creative new ideas for engaging voters and volunteers safely. Still, I got a lot of pushback from my candidates because 'this wasn't how things were done,' but my campaign manager and the older field organizers supported me a lot. It was exhausting having to be so headstrong/stubborn to get an idea that was in the best interest of the candidates to be approved by them." ⁂

"I got a lot of pushback from my candidates because *'this wasn't how things were done,'* but my campaign manager and the older field organizer supported me a lot."

"I learned a lot about campaigns on the job— stuff I never learned in college. I am super grateful for the opportunity. My experience outside the campaign setting was under- valued, despite the new ideas and hard work ethic I brought." ⁂

"It depends very much on where you are, who you are, and how you contribute. I quickly gained enormous control over the campaign's branding, advertising, and messaging, to the point of being named the campaign's co-chair. And with that position, I had a seat at the table on strategy, awareness of spending, interactions with the local party, and other activities. This would likely have been more complicated on a different campaign or elsewhere." ⁂

"One fun thing about working the 2020 primary is that there were so many candi- dates, there were soooo many organizers, and many of us were young, fresh out of college, etc. Looking back on it, I don't feel like I was "one of the youngest" because so many of us were in the same boat.
     On the *Kamala for the People*, the culture was 'if you're good, you're good'— it didn't matter how many cycles you have. For instance, one of our best organizers was a first-time field organizer right out of college. One of our best Regional Organizer Directors had only worked one complete cycle as paid staff before Kamala's 2020 campaign." ⁂

"It's interesting to be one of the youngest because the younger teams tend to win in politics, as we are savvier on social media.
     I also found my youth somewhat restrictive because I needed to gain more experience in some of the more nuanced databases we used, like NGP and VoteBuilder." ⁂

"Most of us were about the same age in Iowa so I don't think it made that big of a difference. The biggest thing is that it led me to being a lot more quiet than I typically would've been only because of my lack of campaign experience. In all honesty, Iowa felt like campaign college. There were tons of people, most of whom were fresh out of college, and we had all moved from all over the country to help win a caucus and eventually beat Donald Trump. It was really cool to be a part of.

Every job I had after the caucus made me think about my age a lot more because I was typically the youngest person in the room. I spent a month organizing in Texas for Mike Bloomberg preceding Super Tuesday and on that team I was the youngest by about 3 years and was probably only one of two or three from a team of 10+ people who was in their 20's.

I spent the last 6-7 months of the 2020 cycle managing two state house races in Iowa and while almost all of us were around the same age, I think I was on the younger side of the group and I was definitely feeling imposter syndrome the entire time." ⁂

"Working with people who had been organizing since I was in grade school was humbling. At first, it was a little uncomfortable feeling like I didn't have any "real world experience" as my coworkers did, but eventually, I could learn from them and develop myself as an organizer and person." ⁂

"I made a really conscious effort to connect with as many people as possible. When you leave college you are leaving this huge network and losing the sense of community that you had for the last for years." ⁂

"It was very helpful to have the opportunity to ask anyone for help since everyone was more senior than me. Sometimes, being the youngest gave me different and fresh insights. That being said, I was very deferential to pretty much everyone in a more senior position— at times, probably too much" ⁂

"I'm a bit older (28 when I started, 29 now), so I always felt too old compared with my colleagues. Obviously, some of the higher-ups were older, but the other field organizers were all younger." ⁂

"It was weird, but expected. I was lucky enough to be on a team where I felt my input was valued despite being so new, but that may have been because my Field Director was a year or two older than I was." ⁂

"On our six-person team, we had two staffers younger than me, one the same age and two older. I was actually in the middle of the pack. I really enjoyed being part of a young, exciting team like that." ⁂

"It can be really intimidating being one of the youngest staffers in the room and can at times feel like an exclusive community. I'm grateful to have worked with some really amazing staff in my state that had predom-inantly female leadership, which definitely impacted my experience." ⁂

"The average age of campaign staff skews fairly young, at least for peer-to-peer and digital organizing. I was usually not the youngest staffer in the room, at 23. While I didn't often feel the typical assumptions that surround being young in an organi-zation, I felt there was an assumption that because you are young, you can do any amount of work being asked of you." ⁂

Q2 / *What's your take on being one of the youngest staffers in the room?*

"Most people on political campaigns are relatively young. What surprised me was how much of a difference I felt there was between being 22 versus being 25 or 26. Even though often my eldest colleague was only about 10 years older than me, it felt really significant in the heightened arena of campaign-land.

I think being the youngest in the room is a blessing (given good management). I felt really lucky to be in the room with experienced campaign vets, learning from them, but also feeling like my ideas were genuinely listened to. This election cycle had a huge emphasis on reaching young voters and I think that's where being in these rooms became really critical—to be the voice saying "no one would say that" or "that would actually be really cringe" helped all of us make more authentic connections with voters. I do caution young staffers if being young becomes a big part of your work identity to be prepared for that to unfortunately, potentially be used against you in later disagreements. I also personally worried that as a young staffer only my ideas about what influencers are cool and what TikTok trends we should hop on would be valued, while my larger strategic ideas would not be. I was lucky enough to have great management where that wasn't the case, but I absolutely believe it's a pitfall young staffers deal with sometimes." ⁂

"The first campaign I worked on had a relatively small and young staff. I sometimes struggled with being so new to the campaign world, whereas lots of the team had been on the candidate's first campaign in 2018 or had previous campaign experience. I often worried that I was missing context or asking more questions than I should have." ⁂

"I was a naive but capable staffer whose heart fluttered upon hearing, *"wow, this is your first campaign? You're composed/calm/acting like you're experienced!"* But at the end of the day, I didn't have robust experience.

I felt a distinct difference between those who saw me as an asset—picking my brain for fresh organizing event ideas versus those who thought I just needed to pay attention to the experts & catch up. Especially when it came to the ups and downs of the campaign trail, I felt that generally, people weren't eager to help fill in the gaps in my knowledge or speak the uncomfortable truths about loss that always were looming, especially in early 2020." ⁂

"Being the youngest staff member in the room was often very challenging. I constantly felt like I had to work harder and longer. Even if other coworkers didn't truly need me to—I had to prove myself over and over. And if I made a mistake, it felt like a much bigger deal and could disqualify me from my position.

In some ways, though, being the youngest staffer was awesome. I learned so much from the people I was working with. My team valued that I came with a perspective that hadn't previously been shaped by working in elections or politics before. I learned to stand up for myself and yell a little louder too." ⁂

"I'm a bit older (28 when I started, 29 now), so I always felt too old compared with my colleagues. Obviously, some of the higher-ups were older, but the other field organizers were all younger." ⁂

"I constantly felt like I had to work *harder* and *longer*. Even if other coworkers didn't truly need me to— I had to *prove* myself over and over.

In some ways, though, being the youngest staffer was awesome. I *learned* so much from the people I was working with."

"One fun thing about working the 2020 primary is that there were so many candidates, there were soooo many organizers, and many of us were young, fresh out of college, etc. Looking back on it, I don't feel like I was "one of the youngest" because so many of us were in the same boat.

On the *Kamala for the People*, the culture was 'if you're good, you're good'— it didn't matter how many cycles you have. For instance, one of our best organizers was a first-time field organizer right out of college. One of our best Regional Organizer Directors had only worked one complete cycle as paid staff before Kamala's 2020 campaign." ⁂

"It can be really intimidating being one of the youngest staffers in the room and can at times feel like an exclusive community. I'm grateful to have worked with some really amazing staff in my state that had predominantly female leadership, which definitely impacted my experience." ⁂

"Ahh! I was (I believe) the youngest full-time employee for my State Democratic Party, and I was really lucky to be surrounded by organizers of all ages who were equally new to field organizing. I felt proud that I was able to provide them my voter protection knowledge and that my percent-to-goal metrics were quite strong. I was glad that instead of hearing "oh my gosh, you should run for president," I was actually respected and valued for my work. Still, I tend to be quite bubbly on video and phone calls so I had a few issueswith male coworkers who did not take me seriously.

However, for the most part, I felt respected and valued. I had multiple people stick out for me to ensure that my pay, union engagements, and schedule were taken care of. I think they knew I was overworked and wanted to ensure I wasn't exploited or drowning." ⁂

Question 3

Do you feel like the campaign(s) you were a part of represented your beliefs?

"In a lot of ways, yes. I think my theory of change was well represented, but I would definitely not call myself a capitalist down to my bones as Warren did. There were times when I wished she would go farther and challenge the imperialism entrenched in our government but I saw her as the best vehicle for the changes that were most urgent and impactful." ⁂

"The campaign and the candidate definitely represented my values, which is what I find most important in these situations. However, my personal policy preferences are very far to the left of the campaign I was working for, and I often had to remind myself of that to stay on-topic and on-message." ⁂

"Yes, on most issues. When joining, I considered myself further left than Kamala Harris's presidential campaign platform. Since the campaign ended, I have become more left-leaning. But for the most part, her policies represented my beliefs. Even if I want more progressive policies, sometimes they do not always resonate with the electorate. I believed in the approach Kamala presented to make change." ⁂

"All of the campaigns I've been a part of have represented some of my beliefs, but not all. I think it's important to relay to young staffers that even when there's a politician who you respect and admire, you will most likely not agree with everything they do and that's normal. I believe in working for the person you feel is best for the job out of the available options." ⁂

"I believe in working for the person you feel is best for the job out of the available options."

*Q3 / Do you feel like the campaign(s)
you were a part of represented your beliefs?*

"I think so, they made an effort to promote diversity and inclusion. I never had a problem with anything the campaign did or said that I felt was against my beliefs."

"I'm further left than the candidates I worked for, but I'm fairly certain that's normal. All of my downballot candidates were progressive, and they are beautiful, impressive, compassionate people who sacrificed so much to fight for us. And up the ballot, while Joe Biden and our new Georgia Senators are not where I'd like them to be, I was proud to fight fascism and voter suppression every day.
I hope Biden and our Senators follow through on their *promises* for *Americans like me* who worked extremely hard to elect them so we could have a brighter future. I cried when our downballot candidates lost, and I cried when we flipped the White House and Senate. I want the work to be worth it." ⁂

"Y. Largely, I was proud to be a part of a progressive campaign. There were, as one might expect, policy preferences and communications choices that differ from my personal beliefs. Usually, that desire was to be more left or to more strongly rebuff certain stances from other candidates." ⁂

"I recently worked for an organization that advocated for progressive issues for the Asian American Pacific Islander community. Being Asian American myself, it was rewarding to really work with a community that is so often underrepresented and overlooked, and that I could help serve and represent my fellow AAPIs with issues regarding immigration, healthcare, education, sustainability, and more." ⁂

"I cried when our downballot candidates *lost*, and I cried when we flipped the White House and Senate. I want the work to be *worth it*."

"In some respects definitely yes. The candidate believed in the importance of a strong federal government, and the importance of providing relief to people because of the coronavirus. Despite this, the campaign itself repeatedly showed to be against many of my beliefs in the treatment of workers and the value of individuals." ⁂

"Like many voters in this country, I felt that there was not much of a choice in this election between the two candidates. From my point of view, one candidate promised ineptitude on the global stage with a side of authoritarianism, while the other, a career politician, promised diplomacy and a response to our growing public health crisis. While I do not go as far to say that I "stan" President Biden, or agree with every policy position he takes, I do believe that he embodies my beliefs much closer than that of former President Trump, in that he values American interests over his own personal ones." ⁂

"Yes and no. The campaigns did align with my beliefs but I will say that there were times that I felt that I was much more progressive/left than the candidates I was working for." ⁂

"No, PTP is a progressive organization in name only. There were a lot of times we were asked to toe the mainstream Democratic line which is not where my personal politics fall. I always kind of wished we supported more robust, meaningful conversations, but the organization prized quantity over quality so I felt like we missed some opportunities to sow greater political engagement." ⁂

"For the most part, I felt that my campaign represented my beliefs. However, the district I worked in was primarily older, conservative white retirees and young, religious families so my candidates had to cater to those beliefs. I appreciated that they did this because I wholeheartedly believe that representatives should actually represent their constituents, but it was difficult to have to curb my own beliefs because my candidates didn't want those stances advertised in fear that it would negatively impact their ratings. We kept a "cheat sheet" of the candidates' stances on major issues so I knew they agreed with my values, but it was difficult to publicly support "truly moderate" candidates who didn't make public statements about pressing and socially relevant issues, like BLM and gun control." ⁂

"No, PTP is a progressive organization in name only. There were a lot of times we were asked to toe the mainstream Democratic line which is not where my personal politics fall. I always kind of wished we supported more robust, meaningful conversations, but the organization prized quantity over quality so I felt like we missed some opportunities to sow greater political engagement." ⁂

"Yes. The district that I worked in during the general election had been flipped blue for the first time in a while in 2018, and the Republican party put tons of money into it in 2020. Because it was so purple, the most crucial thing to me was keeping it blue, even if I disagreed on certain policy points. I never found myself having to advocate for a position that I didn't believe in." ⁂

Q3 / *Do you feel like the campaign(s) you were a part of represented your beliefs?*

"Field staff unionizing should absolutely be the standard. I'm proud to be a part of a campaign staff that made this happen. Coordinated campaigns must live up to their values and support their staff in the future, especially during a national crisis." ⁂

"YES! Beginning July 2020 I worked for Dr. Hiral Tipirneni in AZ-06! I felt as though she truly represented my beliefs and my hopes for Arizona. While there were instances where I have a bit of a more progressive stance, I valued her commitment to a moderate platform, understanding her approach and the realities that exist within Arizona. Sure we may have flipped Blue for Biden but, my-oh-my, we are so far from being a blue state. I must admit working for Jon Ossoff was SO fun for the fact that he's far more progressive and it felt very freeing and empowering!" ⁂

"Yes and no. I worked on one progressive and one more moderate campaign. The progressive campaign was definitely more my speed. The two-party system in the US really encourages and forces people to pick a side, even when the side you pick doesn't reflect what you really believe in." ⁂

"Yes and no. I think was Jaime a great candidate, leader and incredibly talented man. I didn't agree with every policy position the campaign took, but I felt I was working towards a movement that represented the progress I wanted to achieve." ⁂

"I valued her commitment to a moderate platform, understanding her approach and realities that exist within Arizona."

"Yes and no. I personally went through a massive ideological shift over the course of the cycle, so it depends. I entered Biden's campaign as fairly moderate so I was in fairly close alignment with him and his policies when I signed on. Not to say I didn't support what he was campaigning on, but by the end of the race I was far more progressive than where he was at.

Then I'd say that Mike Bloomberg didn't really represent most anything that I believe in, I took that job because the people hiring were promising employment through November. My first priority was employment so I figured that it was the best move for me at the time, something that I can definitely see now was a mistake.

In the state house races I definitely shared the same general feelings as both candidates but obviously it's impossible to exactly agree on every issue. The only time I was actually bothered by the policies of someone I was working for was the month working for Bloomberg." ⁂

"Yes. I cannot say enough how much working on that campaign helped me. It wasn't just Warren's platform, it was the people who worked for her. I was very depressed when graduating and just left very toxic friendships. At Warren, the people there had the same beliefs and interests as me and were beyond kind and respectful. A big thing the campaign taught me was how feeling supported and loved really feels. We supported each other and became a family.

That being said, the actual platform of Warren I felt was the absolute best option for the reality of the electorate. However myself, and many others, are more left than most of the platform. It was disheartening to have the majority of her campaign staff not agree with a lot of her foreign policy plans.

Also, it was really frustrating being on the fundraising team and dealing with the backlash of her saying she'll accept PAC money in the general. While I didn't necessarily think that PAC money in the general, a fight for life or death if Donald Trump would be elected, but we all thought it was extremely stupid that they would reveal this during the primaries. I think it really hurt our campaign." ⁂

"Yes, the candidate is a Democrat and I am a Democrat. I would not work for a campaign who I felt did not represent my beliefs." ⁂

"The work culture of campaigns was not always a part of my beliefs. I'm not very spiritual so in that aspect I don't have much to comment on. But the burnout and overworking culture that is so normalized on campaigns really turned me off from the work. The campaign was having record-breaking fundraising numbers but refused to hire more organizers to give us more time off even though we were unionized and everyone's response was always *"well it's better than it has been in the past so you should grateful."* I have a strong belief in work/play/time off balance and campaigns don't embrace that whatsoever." ⁂

"I would *not* work for a campaign who I felt didn't represent my beliefs."

""In a general sense, yes. The candidate's *overall message* about the unsustainability of suburban sprawl and the need for responsible fostering of the environment was deeply meaningful to me. He brought up many populist challenges to the power of special interests and environmental challenges that are incredibly important for my generation going forward.

I think my candidate had *shortcomings* in his awareness of race relations, especially at the height of *Black Lives Matter* in the Summer of 2020. However, the demographics of the district didn't demand more progressive views. So efforts to raise race relations would have had little strategic value." ⁂

"Yes and no. The campaigns did align with my beliefs but I will say that there were times that I felt that I was much more progressive/left than the candidates I was working for." ⁂

Q3 / Do you feel like the campaign(s) you were a part of represented your beliefs?

"Yes and no. Yes because it was meaning that we wanted to make Georgia better (lol no one cared about us during the general so we had more leeway)." ⁘

"In a general sense, yes. The candidate's *overall message* about the unsustainability of suburban sprawl and the need for responsible fostering of the environment was deeply meaningful to me. He brought up many populist challenges to the power of special interests and environmental challenges that are incredibly important for my generation going forward.

I think my candidate had *shortcomings* in his awareness of race relations, especially at the height of *Black Lives Matter* in the Summer of 2020. However, the demographics of the district didn't demand more progressive views. So efforts to raise race relations would have had little strategic value." ⁘

"Yes, I knew the issues that were a priority for the candidates/committees I was a part of were priorities for me as well. There were a few other candidates where my beliefs were more closely aligned, but it was never a big difference. I really felt *we were all on the same team.*" ⁘

"Yes, I knew the issues that were a priority for the candidates/committees I was a part of were priorities for me as well. There were a few other candidates where my beliefs were more closely aligned, but it was never a big difference. I really felt *we were all on the same team.*" ⁘

"I was captivated by the plans and rhetoric around big bold ideas & structural change on Team Warren. As a student, concepts of learning, taking risks, and reflecting on history were tremendously resonant. I knew the details weren't the most relatable to my leftist politics, but I saw EW [Elizabeth Warren] as the compromise candidate who had potential to listen & grow. I wasn't so interested in my issue-based politics aligning because mine were and remain very fluid as I learn but the campaign priorities— especially the dedication to amplifying Black women organizers—felt more important.

As the presidential cycle went on, I had a harder time relating and spent more time defending the campaign. I felt increasingly at-odds with many personal friends who supported Bernie & didn't have confidence in responding to their critiques. I was constantly on the defensive, worried I was being misaligned as a *"faux-progressive"* like Warren was, and felt a shared grief among campaign colleagues who I saw similarly cornered.

One tough Warren campaign decision that I felt affirmed by was when a senior leader was let go in mid 2020 due to credible allegations of sexual misconduct—to know a campaign would officially take the proper steps and not hide the circumstances was promising leadership & stark contrast to the allegations against the Bernie Campaign in 2016." ⁘

"I think I would say yes. I was lucky enough to work on several primaries where the candidates were progressive just like me. I also worked for a more moderate slate of candidates in the general and while they did not always agree with me on the surface, they wanted to make people's lives better and on that deep, important level we agreed." ⁘

"To have a campaign, but also a candidate, that wanted to *learn* and just do the best they could for every community was a truly amazing experience."

"Both yes and no. The first campaign I was a significant part of was just as a volunteer leader (so obviously a very different experience), which meant that I was sincerely dedicated to the campaign and felt like it represented my beliefs. The second campaign I was hired to work on was less representative of my beliefs, but I knew that going in. I worked on a coordinated campaign in a red state, so the candidates we worked for were much more moderate (which I am not). I did have people on my team who shared my beliefs which made the campaign work easier." ⁂

"If I had to choose between yes and no, I would say yes. I worked for the Warren campaign, for an independent expenditure called Organizing Together 2020, for the Biden-Harris team, and for the Georgia Senate runoffs. I believed that Warren was the best choice for the country, though she had a few policies and some messaging that I wouldn't personally 100% endorse. Biden's policies and values were much further out of line with my beliefs, but it was not difficult for me to get excited about our only chance at progressive change. I joined the Georgia team just a few weeks before E-Day, and I didn't have a deep knowledge of the Senators' platforms." ⁂

"Absolutely. The first campaign I worked on represented my beliefs and point of view on issues more than I ever thought it would. I think part of the reason was because it valued the voices of the community and also of its staff so much that we all had a voice on it. I helped to craft the campaign's policies on climate, democracy, indigenous rights, and more. To have a campaign, but also a candidate, that wanted to learn and just do the best they could for every community was a *truly amazing experience*.

The second campaign I worked on (*Biden for President*) was much different. I found I had to adjust the ways I talked about issues to voters pretty drastically. I often found myself uncomfortable and frustrated to be working for a candidate that I didn't 100% believe in. But it was an important experience too; I found that I could connect to people who had my same ideologies better, and also learned that I need to work for people I feel passionate about in the future." ⁂

"I think I would say yes. I was lucky enough to work on several primaries where the candidates were progressive just like me. I also worked for a more moderate slate of candidates in the general and while they did not always agree with me on the surface, they wanted to make people's lives better and on that deep, important level we agreed." ⁂

Question 4

How did you navigate *and* build meaningful connections in your role with *COVID-19* as a factor?

"As a field organizer, the pandemic presented unique challenges for building meaningful connections with likely voters in my turf. With door-to-door canvassing put on hold, I went to work from my childhood bedroom, dialing 150 York County residents daily and pitching them on Joe Biden. Of my thousands of phone calls, the strongest connections always came with those with whom I shared a piece of myself. Many people were eager to share their struggles and hope for the future once they began to understand why I was doing the job I was doing, and were excited to lend a hand to help." ⁂

"I tried to stay connected with my main volunteers throughout the day by texting them and talking about the day's news. I wanted to get their views on how the campaign was going and understand how they approached breaking news. At the end of the campaign, I had a weekly Zoom call with my volunteer leaders, leading to deeper, meaningful connections. I hope I actually get to meet some of my volunteers at some point." ⁂

"I worked on youth voting primarily, so using my micro-social work skills to meet students where they were at and not just talk to them about getting out to vote but taking the time to have meaningful conversations on voter info and how voting can impact one's life in the short and long term." ⁂

"I'm not sure I built any meaningful connections, which I guess is my failure. I'm still unemployed four months later, so it shows that I didn't make good enough connections which is a lesson I will take with me. I thought I had laid the foundation for meaningful relationships, so maybe I need to reach out. It's hard to ask for help." ⁂

"Thankfully I didn't have to worry about the pandemic during my time on the campaign (as the campaign I was on ended right before the lockdown happened). I was still on my parent's insurance and worked in Massachusetts long enough to get their unemployment benefits, which were much easier to apply for than in other states. I know many people had problems losing their insurance right after the pandemic started. I also wonder how my life working from home would be if I stayed on the campaign trail (I went to work for a nonprofit after the campaign). The in-person office experience made the job for me." ⁑

"It was extremely hard. I was able to build some successful relationships the first time I was in Iowa because of relational organizing. Then when I was managing in Iowa, it was really difficult because I couldn't build new relationships in the same way I had before, and I was also running both teams from a couple of states over in Ohio. I really had to lean on the relationships I had from working on Biden's team and then hope to build relationships through the candidates or other volunteers. It worked out well, as both campaigns had a ton of volunteer capacity for postcards and phone calls. But it was an unbelievable amount of upkeep to manage over 100 volunteer and community relationships, all virtually." ⁑

"When I worked on the Warren Campaign, COVID was not yet as widespread and did not affect my role. At Unemployed Action, COVID relief was the motivating factor. I can't say building meaningful connections was something I worked hard to pursue as I was only consulting part-time and working on law school applications." ⁑

"Within my region, my Regional Organizer Director built bonding activities into our weekly schedule so all the organizers got to know each other. With voters and volunteers, we HEAVILY relied on phone banking and local and county parties helping us co-host events and reach out to Dems in their respective areas." ⁑

"It was challenging without the field office environment: no running to Lincoln Perk with your coworkers for grilled cheese, no hearing others' hard ask or volunteers coming and going. In the general, we tried to have virtual offices where everyone could unmute themselves, ask questions, chat, and build some semblance of a friendship. As for building relationships with volunteers, training them on Zoom was our best way of getting to know them. No having dinners, canvassing, or meeting their friends at the local church. It was very hard to transition from the primaries to the general." ⁑

"There was already a great group of organizers in a few of my counties. I found phone numbers for these people and gave them a call. Our shared hatred for Jim Jordan gave us something in common right off the bat, but then that turned into talking about other things. I grew up in the digital age, so I don't think building connections over the phone was hard at all. For the most part, everyone was kind." ⁑

Q4 / *How did you navigate and build meaningful connections in your role with COVID-19 as a factor?*

"My first role in the 2020 cycle was in person and I *easily* built friendships and connections.

Working *virtually* in my next two roles within the 2020 cycle was definitely *lonely* in comparison."

"My first role in the 2020 cycle was in person and I easily built friendships and connections. I still talk to many of those folks and feel very thankful for that experience. Working virtually in my next two roles within the 2020 cycle was definitely lonely in comparison.

Although we tried to have virtual happy hours/trivia nights to build connections, it wasn't easy. When those campaigns ended, I tried to call and Zoom with as many folks as possible, but it is not the same as knowing someone in-person and seeing them around. Many teammates never even saw my face! I hope to run into them someday in a post-COVID world and figure out we once worked together online." ⁂

"I definitely built meaningful connections through my COVID bubble more than anything. This was a small group of other organizers who had also moved to the state. I also made sure to utilize the connections the campaign made for us with other organizers that became good friends. In addition, I developed close connections with volunteers just through persistent communication and outreach." ⁂

"Our campaign was primarily virtual because of COVID-19, however I still interacted with co-workers constantly throughout the day. I was forced to get very comfortable with talking on the phone and calling people out of the blue. It was also helpful to use Zoom often, for everything from daily meetings to phone banks within the campaign, to voter outreach efforts which connected us with volunteers around the district and country in a much more personal way." ⁂

"A lot of the older staffers in the 2020 cycle might not have realized that Gen Z in the workforce spent more time in Zoom rooms than in-person offices! I feel so lucky that I was able to build really meaningful connections with colleagues while working remotely. I did this by scheduling a weekly "catch-up" FaceTime with coworkers. For me, this weekly Facetimes were a much-needed, albeit not a replacement for after-work drinks or dinners where you'd get to know each other. Other ways included following coworkers on social media, being active in non-work-related Slack channels, and allowing time at the beginning and ends of meetings to talk about personal stuff and just chit-chat." ⁂

> "Gen Z in the workforce spent *more* time in Zoom rooms *than* in-person offices!"

"I struggled a lot with this! I worked remotely for the entire pandemic. My department was small—just four of us. I loved my team and made relationships that I think will last a long time. But I'm social, and I missed daily interactions and the chance to feel a sense of community with people in other departments. Our statewide team had a daily "watercooler" Zoom call for people at the deputy level and higher, so it was manageable and easy to get to know people. I loved this and looked forward to it every day." ⁂

Q4 / *How did you navigate and build meaningful connections in your role with COVID-19 as a factor?*

"I got to know the rest of the field team pretty well, but since the campaign was almost entirely virtual, I didn't get to know the other teams as much as I would've liked. We had weekly staff meetings, and towards the end, we did some in-person stuff, but there weren't the casual conversations that led to real connections." ⁂

"I tried to participate in Slack conversations and spent a lot of time on Zoom. I found that the best way to build connections with volunteers was having a conversation before and sticking around after Zoom phone banks to talk to volunteers about their lives, their pets or kids, and generally just engage in a social activity that isn't possible in person." ⁂

"This was so hard. I was really lucky that my campaign could work in person in offices so I could build incredibly wonderful connections with my coworkers. I struggled a little bit more with my experience with volunteers. Creating meaningful connections over Zoom with technologically challenged folks was not easy. I tried to talk about myself and list when they shared their life stories. I could have done a better job but it seems like it could be okay." ⁂

"With volunteers, I was sure to ask how they were doing and see how their family was holding up—I mostly kept up over text! A volunteer called me right after the President and Vice President were inaugurated to thank me for my work and ask what they could do next—that was really special!

With other staff, I still have friends from the campaign that I have yet to meet in person, and I can't wait for when that's possible!" ⁂

"I tried to proactively schedule casual meetings with people and inject some personality into regularly scheduled meetings. I was able to establish some meaningful connections as a result, but I felt that I missed out on a lot of the relationships I could have formed if this was an average year." ⁂

"Thankfully I didn't have to worry about the pandemic during my time on the campaign (as the campaign I was on ended right before the lockdown happened). I was still on my parent's insurance and worked in Massachusetts long enough to get their unemployment benefits, which were much easier to apply for than in other states. I know many people had problems losing their insurance right after the pandemic started. I also wonder how my life working from home would be if I stayed on the campaign trail (I went to work for a nonprofit after the campaign). The in-person office experience made the job for me." ⁂

"The *in-person* office experience made the job for me."

"A lot of the older staffers in the 2020 cycle might not have realized that Gen Z in the workforce spent more time in Zoom rooms than in-person offices! I feel so lucky that I was able to build really meaningful connections with colleagues while working remotely. I did this by scheduling a weekly "catch-up" FaceTime with coworkers. For me, this weekly Facetimes were a much-needed, albeit not a replacement for after-work drinks or dinners where you'd get to know each other. Other ways included following coworkers on social media, being active in non-work-related Slack channels, and allowing time at the beginning and ends of meetings to talk about personal stuff and just chit-chat." ⁂

"My first role in the 2020 cycle was in person and I easily built friendships and connections. I still talk to many of those folks and feel very thankful for that experience. Working virtually in my next two roles within the 2020 cycle was definitely lonely in comparison.

Although we tried to have virtual happy hours/trivia nights to build connections, it wasn't easy. When those campaigns ended, I tried to call and Zoom with as many folks as possible, but it is not the same as knowing someone in person and seeing them around. Many teammates never even saw my face! I hope to run into them someday in a post-COVID world and figure out we once worked together online." ⁂

"Working virtually in my next two roles within the 2020 cycle was definitely lonely in comparison."

"[With colleagues] we had an open Google-Meets video chat all day long. From time to time, it felt a bit overbearing, but honestly, I would not have been nearly as successful if we hadn't had that office-like feel. [With volunteers] For my volunteer leaders, we ran periodic volunteer leader training with other leaders, so it was a tight-knit group. We also had a Slack channel for our volunteers to help them feel more connected to the campaign, though, to be honest, running a Slack channel while recruiting and running events was a bit too much for us. Additionally, we had a 10-minute debrief period at the end of every virtual phone bank. Debriefing together was key in getting volunteers in. Everyone was sick of Zoom but, at the same time, searching for a connection, and this helped them get that." ⁂

"I was recently a digital organizer during the 2020 Presidential Election cycle, so most, if not all, of my interactions with my team and community, were in the virtual realm. I became accustomed to using programs like Zoom and Google Meet/Duo to have relational 1:1s with people. I also made sure to be more cognizant of how people preferred to connect—whether through video chat, a phone call, or social media. Another thing to note was how impactful it was to follow up with anyone I connected with during my time as a digital organizer; I think it's important to show that the time you spend connecting with others in your community isn't just a one-time deal and to have a meaningful connection needs consistent effort long after an election cycle." ⁂

Q4 / How did you navigate and build meaningful connections in your role with COVID-19 as a factor?

"The relationships that we were able to build on the campaign are still astounding to me. I was fortunate enough to start on the campaign as an intern pre-pandemic. I honestly think [my] relationship with volunteers was stronger during the remote part of the campaign. This may have to do with the fact that I spent more time with volunteers during that time, but I also believe that it was because we were all going through a common struggle. We all looked forward to our time on Zoom calls together in the socially distanced world. I built meaningful connections entirely through Zoom events! We had Zoom phone-banks, Zoom happy hours, Zoom coffee/tea time, virtual house parties, virtual college events, and intern game nights. Zoom, however, isn't always as easily accessible for older members of our community and those without consistent internet coverage. For older individuals, we hosted in-depth training over the phone and via Zoom; it was my utmost priority to ensure volunteers were comfortable with technology and didn't feel like I was just some young person expecting them to use something they were not familiar with. We had extreme success with this and brought our interns in to help with this training. I think that strengthened relationships further because we spent more time with our volunteers and bonded over frustrating technology. I put together LTE writing groups for those without a strong or consistent internet connection. I connected them with writing postcards so they could get involved without using the technology needed to phone bank/text bank virtually. Lastly, I spent much time on the phone with my volunteers. Although it increased my work hours, I let all my volunteers have my personal phone number so they could reach me anytime. I know that many of them weren't used to being unable to go into a campaign office, and I wanted to be, and took pride in being, as accessible as possible." ⁂

"I think remote work was one of the best things that could have happened to me. I thrive in spaces that feel routine, safe, etc. Taking on a very challenging & new job wouldn't have been my first or even my last choice if I was moving away. Remote work allowed me to recognize the support my family and loved ones offer me during days filled with unknowns and looooonnng hours. I have always struggled with anxiety and ADHD, so remaining in a safe space filled with strong routines allowed me to feel comfortable and expand my comfort zone without hitting a breaking point. I have always loved & valued technology. It's not something that scares me.

Perhaps it's [the] fact [that] I went to a technology-based high school, but I have never been afraid of technology. Using Face-Time/Zoom was exciting to me. Of course, I wish I could have met many fellow staffers in person, but I am grateful to consider many of them my best friends. We embraced texting, FaceTime, Zoom, and embraced awkward virtual icebreakers. In the end, what made 2020 possible was working from casual attire, FaceTiming just to work in silence, and sharing T-Swift Spotify playlists." ⁂

"I got to know the rest of the field team pretty well, but since the campaign was almost entirely virtual, I didn't get to know the other teams as much as I would've liked. We had weekly staff meetings, and towards the end, we did some in-person stuff, but there weren't the casual conversations that led to real connections." ⁂

"I honestly think my *relationship* with volunteers was *stronger* during the remote part of the campaign."

"It was very difficult. I live in a different state than the one I worked in, and I never met a single coworker in person. We had happy hours on Thursdays, which was a fun way of talking to people and getting to know them after work." ⁂

"I was too busy attending college virtually, working almost 60 hours a week, continuing to assist with voter protection work, and caretaking to build many friendships.

However, my coworkers and I bonded over meetings, shared training, and insane schedules. We had about half a day off every week, and afterward we'd chat about how it went. One of my coworkers had a precious baby and always showed her off on Zoom calls, and another with a kid my age was also in school (getting her Master's), so we bonded over the fact that after our final meetings at 8 pm each night, we'd both hunker down and do our homework. I love organizers and keep in touch with many of them now." ⁂

"When I worked on the Warren Campaign, COVID was not yet as widespread and did not affect my role. At Unemployed Action, COVID relief was the motivating factor. I can't say building meaningful connections was something I worked hard to pursue as I was only consulting part-time and working on law school applications." ⁂

"With Warren dropping out a week before the lockdowns started, I spent a month trying to salvage what tatters of the campaign network I could cling to before moving on. I was alarmed by how abruptly I stopped hearing from former supervisors but grateful for the push to leave campaign politics and find grounding & stability in my own life." ⁂

"I was alarmed by how *abruptly* I stopped hearing from former supervisors but *grateful* for the push to leave campaign politics and find grounding & stability in my own life."

"ZOOM CALLS ALL THE TIME. It was rare for me to go more than an hour without a Zoom call with either my team or a group of volunteers. I had amazing volunteers who would organize their own call-time groups with friends, and I would make a point to drop in at the start/end of every call and say hello/see how things went. Showing appreciation for my volunteers was a huge point for me. It helped me build great connections with them that I still have today. I also would make an effort to learn something about the voters I was speaking with.

I stopped caring about my call numbers after my first few weeks as an organizer. I made great connections with the voters I talked to and valued that more than a number on a spreadsheet.

With COVID-19 and being in a district with an older population, a lot of voters were lonely and just wanted to talk with someone. One man I talked with at the beginning of COVID told me that his wife had recently passed away. He lived alone and had no human interaction for days until I called him. We talked for 30 minutes and both of us cried as he shared his admiration for our work in politics, he had also campaigned as a young man. Because I was using a dialer system, I couldn't see his phone number but gave him my personal number to call. Richard called me once a week for the next 6 months to see how the campaign was doing and what I was up to in life.

I became a pseudo-grandchild for him, and it was a highlight for both of us to spend a few minutes catching up throughout the summer. Making these types of connections with voters was much more impactful and allowed them to remember me, my campaign, and my candidates better because they actually felt like someone cared about them beyond their political preferences, and that was crucial in gaining the support of a lot of people who were on the fence.

I also used weekly e-newsletters to keep my volunteers engaged. Calling my volunteers every week to hard-ask them into a shift felt ridiculous, and I knew that it would eventually fatigue them. I used my newsletter to provide Mobilize links to our weekly events that the "shift thermometer" to represent how many shifts we needed for the week vs. how many we had. All of my volunteers appreciated this method of communication because they could revisit the information whenever they wanted, and it brought volunteers who took a hiatus from helping back into the fold. The e-newsletter also reduced the number of shift no-shows we experienced because people weren't pressured to say yes to me over the phone so that I would go away without actually attending the event. My newsletter gained traction due to the ease of getting information about volunteering, and I went from sending it to 50 people to 5,000 in a small district" ⁑

Question 5

Were the campaign(s) you were part of effective at reaching out to Millennials and Gen Z voters within the community?

"I honestly don't know. We didn't get the youth turnout we anticipated, but I like to think we made a lot of in-roads in those communities." ⁂

"I want to say yes so badly, but no, not so much. Millennials and Gen Z voters were included in our phone banks, but the campaign's messaging and policies were targeted to GenX and Baby Boomer voters. We did partnership events with local colleges and universities, but encouraging attendance was hard during COVID." ⁂

"No, we did minimal work reaching out to colleges/universities, but I don't recall anything that I would call a success." ⁂

"Jon Ossoff's team did a really good job at reaching younger voters on the internet because there were young people running the digital team there." ⁂

"No. While there was a substantial population of minors, the district's demographics had an enormous population of older voters compared to Millennial and Gen Z voters. We did make limited efforts, particularly on Instagram, but needed more resources to put substantial effort beyond that." ⁂

"Our campaign seemed to have a great campus program to engage the #youthvote. The 'youth' messaging was run separately from the rest of the field work, so I'm unsure how this went. Even before the pandemic, I feel like these cycle organizers used social media more creatively than ever!" ⁂

"No, not at all. We failed dramatically in reaching younger voters. We did not target them, and it was hard to find them. Because colleges were remote, we couldn't interact with college Dems as much as we might have during a normal cycle. Even so, we did not make any effort to get younger people involved" ⁂

"I think so. I was in the field, and most of our outreach with them was digital. I couldn't speak to the logistics of that, but from what I saw, we did a pretty good job. I talked to young people who didn't have their voter registration figured out and assisted them with that, and I imagine plenty of my coworkers had similar experiences." ⁂

"I'm not entirely sure, mostly because the district the race ran in skews older and less connected online. We had really strong outreach with local universities and community colleges and a decent social media following, plus our paid canvass attracted a lot of college-age canvassers, so I'd say it was pretty good outreach with younger people." ⁂

"No. While I believe areas of the campaigns were, the average (peer to peer) volunteer tended to be members of GenX or Boomers. Leadership at the 2020 advocacy campaign I worked on stated in meetings and webinars that the group intended to prioritize unemployed BIPOC. How systemic racism affected the unemployment and pandemic unemployment assistance system caused BIPOC representation not to be reflected in membership.

I remember very few active BIPOC members and those who did participate experienced microaggressions from a white manager who would often 'mix-up' the names of BIPOC staffers. This may have been a contributing factor and shortfall considering Gen Z skews more diverse." ⁂

"Both of the campaigns I worked with had really strong internship programs that got lots of high school and college students involved. The congressional campaign during the general election chased votes starting in September since New Jersey sent out ballots to all active registered voters. We chased every vote, mostly through phones and texts. We helped young people get their ballots turned in." ⁂

"Yes! I was the Statewide Campus Organizer for Massachusetts, so I know for a fact there was an effort to involve young people in the election cycle. I wish we had more resources to provide for students who often didn't have their own cars and couldn't afford merch as many other volunteers could." ⁂

"No, at least not in my area. I did a lot of phone banking to gain volunteers; most people I called were 60+ years old. The youngest person I remember seeing was 21, and she was a rarity. The campaign had a big presence on Twitter, most likely because she would respond to Jim Jordan's tweets. Whether or not these people lived in this district was probably unlikely.

We used the same strategy for every demographic. I think we had one GOTV weekend with a student and teacher phone bank, but that was about it. Most of the interns were college students. But again, the strategy was the same from 18 to 80." ⁂

"I was an intern for Ed Markey and he was an amazing candidate for reaching out to young voters. He reached out to youth so well and honestly had a youth-led campaign all around. However, in my Montana role, I felt like the majority of the people they were trying to reach were older. There was almost no attempt at reaching out to young people on that campaign." ⁂

"I want to say yes so badly, but no, not so much. Millennials and Gen Z voters were included in our phone banks, but the campaign's messaging and policies were targeted to GenX and Baby Boomer voters. We did partnership events with local colleges and universities, but encouraging attendance was hard during COVID." ⁂

Q5 / *Were the campaign(s) you were part of effective at reaching out to Millennials and Gen Z voters within the community?*

"The campaign was very *cautious* at first, but over time *trusted* the younger staffers to carry out youth engagement strategies—and it definitely paid off."

"Unfortunately, I don't think we were as effective at reaching young voters as I wanted to be, though we did try. This is one of my big regrets from the campaign because focusing on young voters was a part of my original role.

One of the challenges with reaching young voters was that our district is fairly older, so we needed to talk to a lot of middle-aged folks and Boomers. Another challenge of our campaign was that the digital organizing team didn't get up and running as early as it should of, and COVID shutdowns threw a significant wrench in our ability to organize young people.

There were a lot of colleges in the area which was the campaign's main way of reaching Gen Z voters. But, shortly after I started, everyone was sent home from school, and we lost that natural network.

I learned that to be effective in reaching Millennial and Gen Z voters, you need to focus on in-person organizing/door knocking, relational organizing, and social media above anything else." ⁘

"Somewhat yes, somewhat no. I was a campus organizer in Iowa, so most of my job was about Gen Z outreach. While we had some really committed and engaged young volunteers, I don't think my candidate (Kamala) was the "youth candidate" during the primary. We didn't have as much engagement as the Warren and Bernie campaigns on campus. But that wasn't for lack of trying or investment. We did have good millennial outreach, and many of our volunteers and biggest supporters were in their 20s and 30s.

At Org Corps, other than digital iorganizing, we only spent a little bit of time teaching youth outreach specifically. I don't think this was a mistake because we trained organizers for all types of turf. Ultimately, [in] the coordinated campaigns the organizers would focus on specific constituency and demographic outreach, whether that be a Gen Z demographic or not." ⁘

"The Warren campaign could have done more to solidify support with Gen Z, but I feel confident that much of the messaging was perfect for a millennial demographic. Sometimes it felt like the campaign was too perfect, with visually flawless events and incredible design, to actually be in on the joke & seen as "policy-first"— how corporate branding is so often used to cover up failings." ⁘

"It was weird, and hard. I tried to do a few 1:1s in Iowa, but those were a lot harder to do post-COVID. It was hard to communicate well with volunteers, and I missed the field office aspect and getting to know my coworkers." ⁘

"The campaign was very cautious at first, but over time trusted the younger staffers to carry out youth engagement strategies— and it definitely paid off. We generated a lot of genuine interactions with young people. I believe the success of engaging with young voters was mainly down to trusting young staffers and their instincts without worrying about the implications of every single interaction or piece of content we put out." ⁘

"During the election cycle, most of my organization's team was of either age group, so yes, I think we were effective at reaching out to the Millennials and Gen Z voters in our communities.

We held phone bank sessions where we only called voters aged 18-25, had GOTV events with themes that would attract youth voters, and created visual content for social media that included various pop culture references." ⁘

"Yes, but we weren't given many resources to make it happen. We had to be creative. My team scraped together and created a voter universe from the ground up using our own Instagram DMs." ⁘

Q5 / *Were the campaign(s) you were part of effective at reaching out to Millennials and Gen Z voters within the community?*

"Honestly, I don't think we had a fantastic "youth" program or program to pull this group in. Many people in this age group were drawn to Bernie, who naturally fit into that space. I think we at Warren did not invest in social media enough. It really pissed me off my entire time on the campaign. There were only 3-4 people on social media, aka one of the (most) essential tools for campaigning. Seeing those people be worked to the bone and stressed out all the time was awful. There were also key spaces on social media where younger people are that the campaign wasn't reaching, like Tumblr (may be dead to some but, boy, was there a lot of politics on there and no Warren presence), Reddit, and TikTok." ⁂

"No. We made cold calls and wrote letters—two wildly ineffective ways to reach young people. Most young people I happened to catch on the phone were either trolling me, were wrong numbers, or had already voted." ⁂

"No. I don't think people really understand how policy-rigid young voters are. None of the outreach they did matters if we're only running moderate, establishment, practically 'Republican-lite' Democrats. Younger voters want to relate to and feel inspired by the candidates that we vote for. Additionally, my candidate's campaign and the party put a lot of emphasis in every ad they ran on her strong relationships with Republicans in the state. I couldn't imagine any young person watching that ad and feeling like the candidate or the party understood them. It was a frequent complaint I heard when I was running a College Dems chapter. The students would say, "I don't really agree with her policy stances, but at least she's not [Republican opponent]." ⁂

"No, at least not in terms of Dr. Hiral Tipirneni's campaign. Arizona's Sixth Congressional District is primarily an older demographic. That being said, we didn't have a high target of Millennial/Gen Z voters to reach out to in general. The campaign's biggest strength was the intern program filled with young people, including several high school students. We successfully targeted young people to become politically engaged and invested by expanding our internship program outside of CD-6 and throughout the U.S." ⁂

"Not especially. I think Democratic campaigns need to up their social media strategy as soon as possible. It seems like the same people who work in social media continue to be hired repeatedly, so we don't see new strategies. The Jon Ossoff campaign was the first that properly used their social media staff and created real, meaningful engagement.

One campaign which I wish had a better marketing team is Elizabeth Warren's campaign. I think the marketing strategy was one of the worst things that happened to Warren, which reduced her reach. It was too broad and not focused—it was too informative. Her marketing team did not pay attention to what the audience needed and would respond to and instead posted what they liked about Warren. And while this approach felt genuine to staff, it caused Warren to be in a weird teacher/professor/elitist box." ⁂

"During the primaries, we intentionally reached out to Gen Z voters in Iowa. However, our campaign failed to swing voters from Bernie to us. Biden did a decent job but nothing impressive." ⁂

"Yes and no. The Biden and Bloomberg teams worked hard to target younger voters, but I don't think they were the focus of any of the work I did on either. I attempted to reach out to younger voters on the Biden team by going to high schools and college career fairs to talk to young people, but it seemed like the caucus format was a pretty large barrier for the young people I spoke with. For Bloomberg, my targets seemed to be predominantly older voters in the short time I was there, so I never really went out to target any young people.

In the two races that I managed, young people were critical to our volunteer efforts. The best intern I had was a high school sophomore from Massachusetts who was one of the Students for Markey. I connected with her through Twitter, and she ended up helping with so much of our digital and organizing efforts. We also tried to connect with all the colleges in the district to try and gain their support; however, due to COVID-19, it was almost impossible to engage with students anywhere in either house district. In Christian Andrews for IA (HD 9), one of the precincts we were most successful in contained a lot of young voters, so it was nice to see that our efforts didn't go unnoticed." ∴

"Eventually, my campaign was effective at reaching younger voters, but my candidates were *upset* that I used new digital ways to do it."

"At first, no. My campaign was very much of the belief that the best way to contact voters was through door-to-door canvassing and phone calls. However, so many younger voters still live with their parents or had to move home due to COVID-19 (like myself) and were inaccessible these ways because their parents would answer the door or they'd be working and unable to answer the phone. And, after business hours, they didn't want to answer the phone/talk politics either because they were tired! I had to advocate for MONTHS to use texting and build an elaborate text program to engage younger voters. My incumbent candidate was very disdainful of it until I showed her proof that it was working.

I used catchy text openings and emojis that people would reply to and say, "I wasn't going to vote, but your text made me laugh, so please give me more information" (one that I was particularly proud of was on Halloween that read: 'It's Halloween and what scares me most is that you haven't voted yet! Do you have a spooky plan for voting in-person or dropping off your mail-in ballot?').

I went rogue trying out new tactics for engaging younger voters (emailing weekly newsletters with information about candidates' stances on hot topics, polling information, campaign goals for the week, etc.; texts; memes on social media; virtual town halls starring my high school interns talking about politics).

The district's record for young voters nearly doubled for the 2020 cycle, yet my candidates refused to acknowledge that these new tactics helped. So yes, eventually, my campaign was effective at reaching younger voters, but my candidates were upset that I used new digital ways to do it." ∴

Question 6

Were there shortfalls in outreach? What are you *proud* of and what would you have done differently?

"Yeah I think the organizing program wasn't as robust as it should be. I don't know a whole lot about on-the-ground organizing, but from what I saw on the digital and HQ side of our organizing staff there were a lot of big egos and very inefficient practices. I don't know how much we could have done better but I think investing in more staff and better staff may have helped. I think we could have prioritized Black, Latino, AAIP, and other identities in our campaign especially since our plans centered around their struggles." ⁂

"If I could go back and change anything regarding our outreach from the campaign, I would focus more on creating content that was hard for people to ignore. It is too easy to ignore a call, or an email, or a text, especially when it is done through cold outreach and lacks the excitement to draw a voter's attention." ⁂

"I'm proud of our ability to think outside the box and use a diverse group of influencers and digital partners to amplify our message in their own authentic voices. I believe authenticity online, especially when trying to reach Gen Z or Millennials, is absolutely critical. I'm proud that we encouraged these creators to make the kind of content they normally would, but were able to work with them to communicate critical campaign messages in a way that felt authentic to them and to their fanbase.

What I would've done differently *drum roll, please* is started earlier and with more money! Unfortunately those are more often than not the issue with building meaningful campaign work, and I feel extra proud of what we were able to accomplish with no budget and on an incredibly tight turnaround." ⁂

"Not providing paid fellowships to bring more working-class young voters into the political process. Again, record breaking fundraising numbers but no investments in areas like paying working class young voters." ⁂

"I was proud of how many people I did end up reaching and talking to even though I was entirely remote. I wish we HAD gone after younger people, especially in my region where we had four or five colleges/universities. I wish that I had taken on interns and taught students how to organize effectively but, again, the campaign did not ever stress the need to bring in college students, at least that I was aware of." ∴

"If I could go back and change anything regarding our outreach from the campaign, I would focus more on creating content that was hard for people to ignore. It is too easy to ignore a call, or an email, or a text, especially when it is done through cold outreach and lacks the excitement to draw a voter's attention." ∴

"I'm glad my role on the Warren campaign came to smooth the gap between the highly produced events & the organizing potential we had at them. We were absolutely on the right track and I would be eager to take on that role again.

I deeply regret not being able to do more for physically disabled event attendees & especially am frustrated by having frequently failed members of the deaf community. I think I did have a scarcity mindset by a certain point though and didn't have energy to continue developing, implementing, and reviewing crowd/community engagement tactics. Advance-organizers could have done so much more if we always had ASL interpreters on staff, networked with local organizers to amplify their work, and had more time to focus on the crowd components instead of event build." ∴

"Yes, there were absolutely shortfallings in outreach, and I think they were the primary reasons for the congressional campaign I worked on losing the election. The two main places were with young people, as I mentioned above, and with the Latinx vote. With young people, COVID-19 was a big factor, as was the fact that we were a rather under-resourced campaign and I simply couldn't spend as much time on that as I wanted to. But the Latinx vote is where I think the campaign really made a mistake. There is a huge Puerto Rican population in the district and our candidate's allyship and advocacy for their community has won him elections in the past. To say the least, it was incredibly important not only for the success of the campaign, but also for the kind of representative our candidate wanted to be to organize in these communities. We would have been exponentially more successful if we'd had a staff member fluent in Spanish and dedicated to making connections within the Spanish-speaking community. It was interesting to realize how young (in terms of electoral organizing experience) our team was. We also worked with advisors outside of the district who didn't know the communities as well and I think that caused us to misspend some resources.

I am really proud of the cross-district coalition and community of volunteers we made. This was a district that hadn't seen a serious challenger in over 30 years and the network of people working for the same goal was truly amazing. We managed to knock [on] thousands of doors safely during a brutally hot summer and a pandemic that kept most people volunteering from home. We were also very effective at building a fellowship program which exponentially increased our voter outreach across the board." ∴

"It took me a lot of time to understand how to balance everything while also accomplishing what I needed to."

"Our dialer budget was cut in the middle of GOTV, for a critical period of time we lost ThruTalk entirely. It was tragic. We had relied on the dialer for weeks if not months and then BOOM the money was no longer there. It was a major hit to our field program, and to our momentum overall, everyone was confused, and it was obviously extremely difficult for our Field Director and her Deputy to not appear concerned/frustrated with the situation. While we got the dialer back eventually it was a scenario that could have been entirely avoided and one that had lasting impacts. It was a time which truly revealed the lack of communication/ respect across departments. Though I loved working on Hiral's race it felt like there were a gazillion fires every day—nearly all of which could have been avoided. While I am incredibly proud for the work we accomplished, the internship program we piloted, the P2P texting program we established, and the passion of so many CD-6 voters, young people, families, and all the rest I wish that communication could have been different. That everyone could at least have a glimpse into the worlds of other departments and above all that we could have all come together instead of tearing one another a part in the midst of tiny fires."

Final random thought: I also think there was a large focus on breaking arbitrary records—oh can we make XXX more calls today—which ultimately led us to diminishing the quality of conversations/outreach overall. It seems that everyone loves these arbitrary numbers but goodness I just wish we could give more time/money to relational and digital efforts which could make the difference instead of relying on outdated systems/numbers that don't always win elections—AZ-06 is a prime example of just that." ⁂

"It felt like there were a gazillion fires everyday—*nearly* all of which could have be avoided."

"Definitely. For me personally, the first issue I had, and I think a lot of people [have] when they start to feel this too, was that it took me a couple months to actually feel like I knew what I was doing. I have no qualms about starting in organizing, but it's a lot of work and it took me a lot of time to understand how to balance everything while also accomplishing what I needed to. Once I worked through my learning curve, I think any shortfall in outreach came from some type of physical barrier to get in contact with someone. For example, if that meant that someone lived in a generally inaccessible area like an apartment building, nursing home, or in a really old town, it was sometimes almost impossible to get in contact with someone. Between all the teams I worked on, I'd say that I'm most proud of the fact that we were able to create teams that did excellent direct voter contact and were always present in meeting the voters where they were." ⁂

"I am very proud of the digital campaign I built through text messages and e-newsletters. I wish that those efforts had been supported by my candidates, but there's nothing I would do differently. I stayed headstrong and stubborn about implementing my ideas (with my campaign manager's blessing, of course) and it made a difference in the election results. If anything, I wish I would have been able to engage my interns in the digital work more, but I didn't want to overload them with responsibilities from an unpaid internship that they balanced with school and extracurriculars." ⁂

$Q6$ / *Were there shortfalls in outreach? What are you proud of and what would you have done differently?*

"One of the shortfallings in outreach that I experienced was that it was harder to reach people in my inner circle to connect with to have a discussion on politics, voting, etc. Instead, it was often people I had been connected to by a mutual friend who were more willing to have a 1:1 with me to discuss such things. I'm proud to have met many unique individuals and form new connections with them. For those that were harder to connect with that I knew on a more personal level, I feel like I should have been a bit more persistent to get to the root of why they were adamant about not being involved in politics.

My organization also had weekly metrics that everyone had to accomplish. For example, make a certain number of calls and hold a certain amount of relational 1:1s. While I had no trouble having virtual meetings throughout my week, it was sometimes hard to meet my metric for weekly calls. I could have spent a few more hours phone banking a couple of days during the week and lessen my amount of virtual meetings. Additionally, there were some calls that I would have that would run well past five minutes. I could have been more assertive with the script or set up an additional call so that that one phone call wouldn't keep me from meeting the average number of calls that day." ⁑

"I think sticking to cold calls only was a huge detriment. I wish PTP would've expanded into an actual digital program and run effective social media pages to help grow their own brand as well as reach younger audiences where they were. I was most proud of conversations that actually divested away from PTP's larger message where I sat and talked to someone for 20-30 minutes. Those conversations always seemed to be the most effective." ⁑

"I wish the work of BIPOC organizers was given more than virtue-signaling lip service. I wish it was valued. I wish the leaders of teams looked like the people who often do the brunt of organizing work. I believe starting from this point is essential in asking questions about outreach. To put it simply, certain leadership are simply not versed on how to begin to credit BIPOC, create the space for them to thrive, or meet their needs." ⁑

"There were definitely shortfallings in outreach across different groups. I was proud of our rural outreach work, but the urban and suburban outreach just did not seem like we reached the people we needed to." "There were definitely shortfallings in outreach across different groups. I was proud of our rural outreach work, but the urban and suburban outreach just did not seem like we reached the people we needed to." ⁑

"I wish the work of BIPOC organizers was given *more* than virtue-signaling lip service."

"I'm really proud of how our campaign was able to educate phone bankers and voters on a totally new voting system. By November 3rd at 8pm, we really had chased every vote, and as things got closer after Election Day, we executed a really strong ballot cure program. I think that we could've started ballot cures sooner, but since the race had originally been called on election night, it took a bit to realize how close things were getting as ballots were counted. During the final 2 weeks, we also did some in-person lit drops/canvasses in a few towns that we saw fewer ballot returns and phone conversations in. I think these were well-executed, but led to some confusion because they weren't part of the initial plan." ∴

"I was proud of the relational training I created and sent to some friends working on the campaign. I think that the push to use relational organizing in Montana was such a good idea for isolated communities. I think that I would have shown up to more community events that were safe like farmer's markets and park events. I think that showing up [in-person] in the community could have actually made a difference." ∴

"Being in Miami, there was a lot of concern about how to get messages out to the mono-lingual Spanish community. It's an issue we worked on throughout the campaign but still were unable to see the success with that group that we wanted to. As we saw in the election results, that was a problem with other orgs as well. In retrospect I'm not sure how much could have been done on an organizing level—the cultural and ethnic politics of the area are so deeply set that it'll take more than one cycle of organizing to fully and adequately address them." ∴

"Yes, absolutely. I am sure you know what Jim Jordan's district looks like; it's not pretty. I live in Allen County, OH, which is in the body of the duck. I was given five counties (Allen, Auglaize, Shelby, Logan, Champaign) and a sliver of another (Mercer). I was only supposed to work 20 hours a week. I am one high school student. There is no possible way that I could contact voters in all of these counties, working only 20 hours a week. It takes so long even to get one volunteer, let alone a few volunteers in each county. We were supposed to have signs and post-cards out in early September, and it ended up being early to mid-October. It seemed that everything was late. I got postcards to distribute to volunteers, but I did not have any postage to send them out until a few days before the election. I am most proud of how I went from a volunteer to an intern to a field organizer in just a few months. It was part circumstance, but there were also other interns they could have picked, and I was chosen instead. I showed my excellent work ethic, and I was rewarded for it. I hinted at this a bit in another question, but I wish I were more assertive. There were also times when I needed things, and I let them go. People continued to say they would get me something, but it took days or sometimes even weeks. I did not want to be pushy, but I also needed things to be done." ∴

"Our outreach was really great, but I wish we could have door-knocked more. It's unfortunate that COVID got in the way of knocking [on] doors, and I wish we could rerun the campaign in a safe zone where we could go up to doors and meet with people in person." ∴

"The campaign's biggest challenge was having the funding to conduct outreach. At the time of the election, the local party did not have a strong organization, and although they provided some funding, did not provide the team effort we hoped for, despite this being the highest-level local race of the cycle. We were unable to substantially encourage opposition voters to reconsider, with broadly party-line voting across the board in the election. We witnessed an incredible amount of disinformation about our candidate, our party, and broader social issues that we did not have the resources to counter effectively. Despite that, I am proud of the work we did to raise the profile of the party, and ultimately shift the winning candidate to support some of our ideas.

We did a decent job of facing a hostile opponent in a hostile area, and presenting a strong face for our party, with serious ideas about our district's challenges. We designed an enormous amount of content for supporters and opponents to spread our ideas as far as we could, and through that effort outperformed candidates in other races." ⁂

"I can't identify any shortfalls in outreach, aside from the inevitable accessibility issues that come when you can't do in-person events. We (organizers, interns, and volunteers) worked our asses off to make sure that we reached as many people as possible. Volunteers and interns would make extra calls, hold phone banks with their friends, text bank in their spare time, and make volunteer recruitment calls when lists were exhausted in whichever phase of the campaign we were in. Our campaign and our district was a village and we truly all worked together (virtually) to get the job done. At the end of it all there were no regrets. We truly left it all on the field." ⁂

"Our campaign didn't do outreach to minority communities. One reason I was given was that since the coordinated [campaign] was only up and running for 3 months, we didn't have time to build genuine relationships. My region ran a Spanish-language phone bank, but in order to get the list we had to jump through several hoops and not tell certain higher-ups. I was proud of the fact that we had volunteers from out of state. Our state isn't one that folks were trying to swing, so to have a good enough program to attract and maintain [out-of-state volunteers] was fantastic." ⁂

"There were shortfalls for us because as a mechanism within the state party focused on state legislative races, we did not have wind in our sails when it came to messaging. Voters didn't know why these races mattered, and I don't feel we did enough work to inspire and educate them." ⁂

"I am proud of the work we did to raise the profile of the party, and ultimately shift the winning candidate to support some of our ideas."

"I am from the South and felt like there was a lack of understanding or focus on non-urban hubs. The 'average American' families that don't come from the privilege that a lot of staffers come from." ⁂

Q6 / *Were there shortfalls in outreach? What are you proud of and what would you have done differently?*

"I wish we had spent less time trying to reach ticket-splitting voters who were going to go for Trump and Jaime [Harrison]. I understand the strategy, but I think it is better in the long run politically to have a campaign that will be really openly critical of a Republican President, even if he's popular in the state." ⁜

"I wish we had spent less time trying to reach ticket-splitting voters who were going to go for Trump and Jaime [Harrison]. I understand the strategy, but I think it is better in the long run politically to have a campaign that will be really openly critical of a Republican President, even if he's popular in the state." ⁜

"In my roles we made it a priority to execute outreach that included every voting demographic, from ethnic groups to LGBTQ+, religious groups, women, etc. I think that it was understood that we needed everybody for this cycle, and that every vote genuinely counted. Diversity is the biggest strength the Democratic party possesses." ⁜

"I do not feel that either the Kamala campaign or Org Corps had significant shortfallings in outreach. I was really proud of our constituency outreach and work on the Kamala campaign. What I would have done differently is pushed even harder for a paid internship/fellowship program in the fall as I think it would have helped with student engagement." ⁜

"The Warren campaign as a whole (not IA for EW), failed to sell our message to young voters and the Muslim vote. I'm proud of the outreach we did for the caucuses: half of my precinct leaders were first-time voters who were excited and doing important community work.

For the general, I'm proud of the work Susie Lee's team did for AAPI and MENA voters. I held events targeting the Persian population and the Asian American population with our Boba and Ballots event." ⁜

"I think we could have done better outreach to API and Latino communities has underperformed in turnout relative to heavily Republican precincts." ⁜

"I doubt that we did everything perfectly; I assume there were some shortcomings in each campaign. My work didn't focus much on outreach, except when I was an organizer on the Warren campaign and responsible for volunteer engagement. I thought the Warren program was strong, but I think electoral politics volunteering, as opposed to deep organizing and community movements, is inherently pretty limited." ⁜

"I think it's hard to say during COVID, especially since this was my first campaign as a paid staffer it was hard to tell whether or not we were successful." ⁜

"We can't win if we only show up around an election."

"I was very proud of how strong our phone banking program was, but we were in a state that has seen no long-term investment by Dems, so it was a little hard to bridge that gap. *We can't win if we only show up around an election.* I think that the state party should have invested in local and county parties a lot more and we need to make sure we have year-round organizing programs so people know that Democrats are here working and a viable option. One of the women we were running for Congress told us that the hardest part about running for office was talking to voters who said something along the lines of *"Well I really like you and your policies, but I'm not going to vote because I don't think that the Democrat can win."* Democrats not investing in red/purple communities helps create cynical voters. Creating voters that are cynical who don't believe that change can come is one of the most effective forms of voter suppression. As a party, we need to invest everywhere. *We will never recreate Georgia unless we invest in red and purple communities.* But outreach to red communities does NOT equal only running moderate, centrist Democrats." ⁙

Question 7

What were the largest *barriers to success* within your role(s)?

"The communication within my first team was strained. There was a hierarchy problem because the team had two different focuses, and our manager was fired in the early fall. The communication problems were solved by dissolving the team." ⁂

"In the general, I had too much on my plate as a Political Manager and Field Organizer. I should not have had to work 2 jobs— DCCC did a poor job of handling my role. I organized multiple events every week, drafted memos, and maintained volunteers while coordinating and collaborating with 10 groups. It was all-consuming.

My bosses knew I had *too* much on my plate. It felt chaotic and like I was constantly failing." ⁂

"Honestly, I loved my job. Jaime was incredible. My team was incredible. I don't know what I would have changed." ⁂

"[As a field organizer,] simply getting people to pick up the phone! Most folks don't pick up from numbers they don't know these days." ⁂

"[As a digital staffer,] how slow the political field can be to adapt to current digital strategy felt like a barrier. It can be frustrating when you have to convince people even to try a tactic that the corporate space has proven effective for years. It is also hard to feel that you're set up for success when trying a new strategy when you don't receive the resources necessary to make it happen." ⁂

"I spent part of this cycle working in the Training department, which I loved. I was so grateful to be on a statewide team where training was a crucial part of the campaign's strategy.

Sometimes, I worked to support other departments' training needs and was overwhelmed by the depth of their need. The folks were really overworked, and understaffed." ⁂

"[As a field organizer,] it sometimes feels like everything is a barrier to your success. One of the primary aspects of the job is to find people at home, either in person or by phone, and then talk to them about their political beliefs. That's just never going to be easy, and you're sort of always at the mercy of the kindness and tolerance of total strangers.

Once I realized that there was nothing I could do to control whether or not people would open the door and instantly start screaming at me, it became easier to deal with the various reactions I would get. Another barrier as a field organizer, in my opinion, was that because you're at the very bottom of the chain of command, I had a lot of times where it felt like everyone was constantly piling on and telling me what to do. Once I could confidently believe that I was doing everything in my power to do my job to the best of my abilities, it was easier to deal with all of that.

As a manager, I also felt anything any day could be a barrier. Whether that's a disagreement with the candidate, other staff, or the voters themselves—I felt there's always something that isn't going to be ideal, and it is my job to fix it as soon as possible." ✮

"[As a Field Organizer,] COVID was a massive barrier. Making meaningful connections with voters is hard when you can't talk to them face-to-face." ✮

"The biggest hurdle for me was being stretched so thin. We didn't have a lot of time to develop good long-term plans or new methods for email production.

We did pretty well with developing testing plans. When we finally had time, normally, I was burnt out, or there was a fire to put out." ✮

"As a field organizer— I had a lot of times where it felt like everyone was constantly piling on and telling me what to do."

"The biggest challenge I ran into was a lack of clear direction/concise communication. There were days in which I felt micromanaged for silly tasks like sending an email, leaving me without time to breathe or think straight. But then there were periods of time in which I was lacking clear instruction/goals—there was never a fully developed plan, just bits and pieces getting attention randomly. More than anything I think the biggest challenge Dr. Hiral Tipirneni's campaign faced was trust—most notably between the Campaign Manager & Field Director. No one communicated effectively; instead everyone assumed things could be done or snapped when things weren't as they had expected etc. I think the distrust created a huge amount of tension which ultimately affected everyone including our part-time field interns. Everyone was living in fear of being screamed at or messing up but not intending to etc. The distrust only continued as rumors spread like wildfire. That being said, the largest barriers to being successful were clear communication and a positive team culture." ✮

Q7 / *What were the largest barriers to success within your role(s)?*

"I couldn't take the time to *process* or address my mental health because I was working *12 hours* a day, 7 days a week."

"[As a campus organizer], the lack of time off we received and being able to take care of my personal needs and mental health. Once our 1-day off was taken away, I did my best to get through each day, but I was in the midst of an intense depressive episode. I couldn't take the time to process or address my mental health because I was working 12 hours a day, 7 days a week. Another one of the biggest challenges was not being able to offer compensation to campus fellows. It was hard to ask the students to give me 15+ hours a week of volunteer time and not address their economic security needs. The campaign messaging of "if you don't work hard enough and Trump becomes president, you can reflect on that later" was very toxic to all of these aspects." ⁂

"I was a field organizer in 2020. COVID-19 was the biggest barrier to building community, organizing effectively, and being a good organizer in 2020. What has not been said about this? I wish I could have spent time in living rooms, coffee shops, and parades. I wish I could get a do-over without COVID. *Doesn't everyone though?*" ⁂

"The team I was working on was very understaffed when I joined and it made proper training very difficult. Early on I felt like I was flying blind but that the more senior members of the department (there weren't many) didn't have time to guide me. This was exacerbated by COVID conditions because it's much more difficult to get a sense for what is going on inside an organization when you can't pick up cues from what's happening around you. All communication has to be very intentional, and when people are very absorbed in their jobs it's very easy to slack on communication, as important as it is." ⁂

"The campaign structure and tasks I was assigned with were some of the biggest barriers to being successful.

We had consistently high goal numbers, leading to less meaningful interactions while canvassing. The work was hitting goals. Instead of building a network of different groups and people that would last beyond the campaign, I was mostly tasked with finding people who would volunteer the most." ⁛

"I, along with the two other women on the campaign, noticed being treated differently by some male staff members. Our organizing team was one woman in her 50s, a male organizing director and myself.

It was often frustrating to bring up ideas and have them disregarded at the moment, just to be repeated back as 'new' three weeks later.

I remember countless moments of being overlooked, shut down, or talked at beyond belief. Having another woman on the team to vent with was a lifesaver. It was constantly working for something I really believed in that got me through." ⁛

"I started on a started on a coordinated campaign as a field organizer in July 2020. My region did not have a Regional Organizing Director. I had to be my own Regional Organizing Director and help some of the older staffers with being organizers. My region then underwent 6 different RODs until September, when we finally got a permanent ROD. That was tough, but it made me more self-sufficient and more of a self-starter." ⁛

"I found it difficult to create a strong intern program because the teams and who was responsible for the program changed throughout in the general [campaign]. The Field and Mobilization Directors provided consistent leadership, but the Field Organizer's direct supervisor changed before GOTV, and led to confusion about what was expected from the team.

The virtual environment also made things hard because everything was a phone call. We always choose to risk having too much volunteer contact over not having enough, but I think that when you aren't the one on the phones, it's easy to underestimate how getting too many phone calls can mess up the volunteer experience and make people less willing to help. We also faced competition from other equally worthy causes, so we constantly had to remind/convince volunteers that it was important to keep this seat blue." ⁛

"A campaign mostly remote was hard. It's more of an emotional barrier, but being a field organizer during a pandemic was difficult to tap into the sense of community. Uncertainty is also normal in campaigns, but the pandemic added another layer of uncertainty. That was really hard to grapple with." ⁛

"The district of large, coordinated campaigns coming in, building infrastructure, using local volunteers, and then leaving the minute the campaign was over.

I could tell there was a deep level of distrust between the campaign and the constituents while working with a coordinated campaign." ⁛

$Q7$ / *What were the largest barriers to success within your role(s)?*

"The largest barrier to success in voter protection work was dealing with underfunded county elections offices. When curing ballots—especially for disabled and new voters—our biggest hurdle was getting county elections offices to do their part in time.

In the field, the biggest hurdle was our flake rate. There wasn't enough time to finish work, and even when we made all our calls, the flake rate was demoralizing. I had a pretty strong recruitment and completion rate, but it was still depressing for us as organizers trying to connect with our volunteers." ⁘

"Over-organizing. The first campaign I worked on, worked too hard to reach people to the point of being a nuisance. I think it's important for campaigns to remember that while confirm calls are super important, seven rounds of confirm calls in a day is ridiculous.

Most U.S. voters are trained to believe that their civic duty is to show up at the polls and nothing else. Of course, it's important for voters to be a little more involved, and organizing makes a difference, but pushing people to volunteer too much hurts campaigns. I saw it happen firsthand.

As a first-time organizer, I used persuasive tactics to convince voters to volunteer. And the tactics worked, and I was able to build a solid volunteer base. However, I was often pushed to repeatedly call and contact people who did not want to participate with campaigns, even though they had refused on multiple occasions. Our campaign lost their votes because of this. Campaigns should find a happy medium between persuading voters to volunteer and persuading voters to just vote." ⁘

"[As a digital organizer,] language was one of the largest barriers. Unfortunately, I am not bilingual, and many of the constituents I had to contact often spoke limited or no English. It made me more aware of the importance of expanding language accessibility for our voters.

Additionally, my organization specifically canvassed the Asian American Pacific Islander community in our state, but politics is usually a contentious topic for this population. It was common to contact a constituent from the AAPI community and have them negatively react when we tried to engage with them about voting and progressive issues. There was also a barrier in terms of age; it was often easier to connect with AAPI youth than with older AAPIs." ⁘

"[As an event organizer on the Warren campaign], I was constantly undermined by advance staff whose priority was visual cohesion & logistics. The way colleagues, volunteers, and event attendees were tokenized based on appearance still upsets me. I often felt like my role was harm reduction—trying to put out the fires that racist/ableist/ignorant staffers started—rather than seizing opportunities to organize events." ⁘

"Lack of knowledge. When I came in as a field organizer, I needed to figure out how to achieve my goals. We had an onboarding, which gave an overview, but the day-to-day of how to actually do my job was something I struggled with initially.

My Regional Organizing Director was very good at always being available to answer questions, but I just genuinely didn't know what questions to ask. My Regional Organizing Director had been campaigning long enough that they no longer remembered what they needed to learn early on." ⁘

"Pushing people to volunteer *too* much hurts campaigns.

I was often pushed to *repeatedly* call and contact people who did not want to participate with campaigns.

Our campaign *lost* their votes because of this."

Q7 / *What were the largest barriers to success within your role(s)?*

"*[On Warren for President]* I have a disability. I have several. While I'm unsure if my work product suffered, my mental health certainly did. Working 80 to 90-hour weeks is not something I would or could do again.

My desire to prioritize my health, made impossible by 80 to 90-hour work weeks, was a source of tension for team members who were focused on judging their success, the campaign's success and how many hours they spent in HQ.

Asking for and taking accommodations (which didn't fit my needs usually, e.g. starting the day at 8 am instead of 6 am on caucus day) were also sources of tension. The HQ campaign environment affected my condition and took away any personal desire for success. My goal was often to get through the day without crying." ⁂

"[As a Field Representative], being limited to two archaic communication modes was a barrier. Writing letters and making phone calls are great, but we should have used those methods with other communication modes like texting, emailing, and other social media outreach. There wasn't a ton of freedom given to Field Representatives, which ended up being a detriment. We were the youngest part of the team and had an ear to what motivated young people to vote and participate in politics more generally." ⁂

"Honestly, I loved my job. Jaime was incredible. My team was incredible. I don't know what I would have changed." ⁂

"The largest barrier was simply inexperience when I was a Field Organizer; I had to learn how to work with the databases campaigns use as well as the logistics familiar to local campaigns (i.e. how to work with the local party, supporters, volunteers, and unions, etc.)." ⁂

"Once I became a field organizer, the largest barrier to success was training. The field organizer who I worked under as a volunteer and an intern was incredible. She sat me down, and we had an hour— or two-long training where she walked me through everything. She was one text away if I needed anything at all, and she never hesitated to help me. However, once I became a field organizer, it was like I was on my own. I had to figure everything out by myself. I have a mutual, and she worked on AOC's campaign, so I reached out to her for help when I needed it. I was very thankful to her. She gave me more support than people on the campaign [where I worked]." ⁂

> "There are *only* so many hours in the day, and it was *difficult* at times to be available for the campaign."

"As a Field Organizer on Kamala for the People, I didn't feel like I encountered any significant barriers to success other than wishing my candidate was more popular in my very progressive turf.

As a Pod Leader, having two full-time jobs in tandem, organizing my turf, and managing three other organizers directly, was a huge barrier.

The biggest barrier as an Organizing Corps Coach was the pandemic. It was challenging to train people to organize in a location I had no experience in and had never been to. At least if it had been in person, I would have traveled to the state/ turf for the trainings." ⁂

"Time and money. There are only so many hours in the day, and it was difficult at times to be available for the campaign, and complete some of the efforts we needed. Running the first partisan challenge for this position, while rejecting support from special interests meant depending mostly on small donors, which presented fund-raising challenges. There was only so much money we could spend on our race." ⁑

"I think the largest barrier was the nature of working remotely. Every morning I'd get up, work out, make breakfast, and clock in for the morning meeting. After that, I'd make calls and send texts for the day until my day was over. Doing this while living by myself and not seeing anyone in person was hard, in the sense that bringing the energy by yourself is a lot more difficult than working on a campaign in person and being able to feed off the energy your coworkers provide. Also, interacting with potential voters exclusively in a remote setting was tough. It's way easier to connect with someone in person and form a bond than it is to call them over the phone and do so. I understand why remote work was necessary (with all of the COVID risks), but in-person conversations are way more effective in my opinion." ⁑

"I was a field organizer for my campaign. The largest barrier I faced was my candidate. It was to the point where it felt like they were attempting to self-sabotage their campaigns because they were so resistant to change and making modifications to their campaign strategy to accommodate COVID restrictions. Because it was a local campaign, the team was small (5 paid staff, including the campaign manager and 14 unpaid high school interns). The candidate was very involved with monitoring our work.

Most of my time was spent building spreadsheets to document and *"prove"* to the candidates that we were working when we said we were rather than making voter contact.

It got to the point where one candidate became so distrustful of us [on] the campaign staff that we were forced to work in-office despite our contracts stating we would be remote until the pandemic had subsided and it was deemed safe to have an office at full capacity.

Being micromanaged took away productivity and lost respect amongst staffers for the candidate. The candidate also started shutting the field team out by removing field-work tasks (i.e. creating mailers and walking canvass packets). Our volunteers knew more about the process than the staff did. It was incredibly frustrating to deal with the candidate's insecurities that caused this situation." ⁑

Question 8

Were you treated differently because your identity *(gender, race, sexuality, etc.)*? How did you cope with mistreatment?

"I identify as a straight, white, female, and I personally do not feel that I was ever treated differently. We had strong teams of powerful women and I felt empowered with my team." ⁂

"I think definitely, especially in rural outreach a lot of our women and POC organizers were not able to be as successful as I was because of their identity. It is much easier for me to code switch and fit in with those in rural areas as a straight white man." ⁂

"I had two unrelated incidences where a direct supervisor made antisemitic comments. The first time I didn't mention it to the director, but after the second one, I decided I had to. I spoke up because the comments were made in front of Jewish interns who might not feel comfortable doing so. The director was very receptive and supportive." ⁂

"I am certain I was treated with the inherent privilege that comes with being a straight white man. Jaime's team had excellent diversity in race, sexual identity, and background. I felt like it was a really cohesive team that supported and encouraged a diversity of thought, but I am positive I benefited from a privileged identity." ⁂

"I was looked *down* upon as being *too young* and inexperienced to have valid ideas to contribute..."

"I had two unrelated incidences where a direct supervisor made antisemitic comments. The first time I didn't mention it to the director, but after the second one, I decided I had to. I spoke up because the comments were made in front of Jewish interns who might not feel comfortable doing so. The director was very receptive and supportive." ⁝

"During the few in-person events that were held or the few in-person meetings I had, everyone was very kind to me.

The campaign held many text banks. In one county specifically, there were a lot of horrible comments that were sent back to me. I understand why. People get a lot of texts from different organizations, which can be annoying. People also do not realize that a real person is behind some of the messages.

There were a few instances where I got some very unwanted sexual comments and even a picture back. I lied, saying I was a minor (I had just turned 18, but it doesn't make it any less wrong or weird), then they apologized." ⁝

"I was treated differently because of my age. I was looked down upon as being too young and inexperienced to have valid ideas to contribute to the campaign plan and was often shut out from strategy conversations. I handled this by speaking with the older field organizers who in turn advocated for me to the campaign manager and candidates. By the end of the campaign, I stopped caring about the potential of being fired for not complying with being silenced and would merely mention to my team what I was doing, the thought process behind it, and then return with the results after I was finished. That stopped the candidates from speaking down on me in front of me and they began talking about it with the campaign manager who took all of it and continued to advocate for me and my ideas." ⁝

"—in rural outreach a lot of our *women* and *POC* organizers were not able to be as successful as I was because of their identity."

"Yes—because of my gender. Another female-identifying field organizer and I inevitably ended up doing more work than our male colleagues. I was never asked to do more work, but when shifts needed to be closed or other things wrapped up outside of work time the male-identifying field organizers were more likely to bow out. It's not like they never did it, but my female co-field organizer and I definitely did more than our fair share.

Similarly, the men on our team had multiple emotional outbursts that they were coddled through. If one of the female field organizers got heated for one reason or another, we would be lightly teased about it by male field organizers before being signaled to suck it up (never in so many words)." ⁝

"I did not feel that I was treated differently because of my identity in either of my roles." ⁝

"I'm not sure. I'm a Black woman and I did deal with toxic co-workers, so I'm not sure if it was because they were being racist or because they were an asshole. I coped with it by venting to a co-worker who understood my frustrations. Being listened to and understood kept me from spiraling." ⁝

"I did notice that my BIPOC friends did feel *alienated* and not heard most of the time."

"I do not feel I was treated differently because of my gender, sexuality, or religious affiliation. I felt supported in an all-female team. I made lots of queer friends. The time off I needed for religious activities was always respected.

I did notice that my BIPOC friends did feel alienated and not heard most of the time. While the campaign said that it believed in equity, there was often not enough implementation of equitable and anti-racist treatment." ⁂

"I personally did not feel treated any differently in my job on the campaign. A lot of the mistreatment and discomfort I felt was because I was a Warren supporter. I mainly felt a lot of sexism from Bernie supporters who were so unwilling to see how she is an asset to the Left and their politics aren't that different. Also new coverage of Warren felt slighted because she was a woman. It made me look at my womanhood a lot more closely and realize how much sexism exists. I started feeling very uncomfortable around straight white men because of the way they treated me for being on the campaign." ⁂

"No, I was not treated differently due to any parts of my identity." ⁂

"Yes & no. I wasn't mistreated but I did see how my male colleague felt after hearing time & time again, "This is why I believe in female strong teams," "We love girl power," "Guys are the worst etc. except for so & so". I had never seen anything like it before and maybe they didn't have bad intentions but I saw how uncomfortable it made the only paid male field staffer. Additionally, I felt weird...I didn't agree with it? It was just odd & left the male field staffer feeling like a dick when really he was just lumped into dumb male stereotypes." ⁂

"Not by my superiors, but I definitely experienced racism and sexism while organizing from my turf. Working in a 90%+ white region as a POC was a weird experience. There wasn't much support from my superiors, but there was support from my fellow organizers. I don't think I would have been able to take as much as I did without that organizer support." ⁂

"Personally I did not notice any different treatment. As a woman in politics I did have many female role models in leadership roles to look up to, and who I know would have advocated for me if there had been a situation that needed it. This is only speaking for myself as a white woman in a position of privilege. We did a lot of DEI (Diversity, Equity, Inclusion) training across each of my roles and others spoke up about their experiences, which helped me understand how spaces on campaigns can be made more inclusive." ⁂

"I do not feel I was treated differently because of my identity, which I recognize is the privilege of being a white woman in this space." ⁂

"The racism that my Black colleagues—*especially Black women*—faced similarly still haunts me."

"I was one of the first and only trans or nonbinary staffers based out of the Warren HQ. I could write a book on the abject disregard I felt most colleagues had toward me & my identity. I found community with state-level organizers and love the non-binary community we maintain to this day. I was particularly uplifted hearing several say they were not experiencing such hardship in their own community organizing & honestly that carried me through my work. But that doesn't change the number of times I cried myself to sleep after game days where I was misgendered & disrespected by campaign staff. Even before I was on staff, I lamented to HR the lack of support for trans people in the campaign and was told "maybe I should be more considerate of those who don't understand (my) gender." While something like pronouns being in Twitter bios & email signatures eventually became standardized, everyone gave themselves a pat on the back & moved on—never asking sincerely how that impacted people like me or what practices would support me.

The racism that my Black colleagues—especially Black women—faced similarly still haunts me. The disregard some white women had for my friends was incessantly on display & only when it became a national news story (when several Black women state staffers publicly resigned) did senior leadership name it as a problem. I was glad to talk about those tensions with my affected colleagues but did not know how best to support them besides identifying specific actions that were unacceptable & offering space for them to vent." .:.

"Certainly. As I mentioned earlier, disability played a huge role in how I was seen and this certainly was compounded by my race (I'm Black). While white staffers were seen as suffering and were allowed to take a weekend to visit their significant others, I was judged harshly for whatever meager accommodations I received and once subjected to being walked out on by a coworker for simply suggesting I would take my assigned day off rather than show up in case of a hypothetical 'crisis.' There was often a feeling of hostility on my team. This was often because white staffers would hurl work at me and the other Black woman on the team, having us pick up for them for their convenience (e.g. so they could take an earlier bus home) without asking first, simply assuming we were available, and approaching us to do this extra work through private messages rather than on the team channel. I didn't have the time or physical space to cope with this. It got to the point where I would go to the phone booths in the basement to avoid the hostile attitudes. The way I felt has fundamentally shaped my desire to keep away from campaign spaces. The kinds of overwork and the racialized perceptions that lead to that overwork were also felt on my other campaign. Specifically, being talked down to, called the names of other WOC (though this occurred on both campaigns by different people), and having to explain racism and issues stemming from racism to coworkers though it was not my job to." ⁂

"There was often a feeling of *hostility* on my team.

The way I felt has fundamentally shaped my desire to keep *away* from campaign spaces."

"I am very privileged as a cisgender white woman who presents as straight, so I never felt particularly singled out.

After the Warren campaign, I went on to work as a state data director at *NextGen America*—and even in that more male-dominated space, I never felt like anyone was questioning my presence." ⁂

"I, along with the 2 other women on the campaign, noticed being treated differently by some male staff members. Our organizing team was one woman in her 50s, our male organizing director, and myself.

It was often frustrating to bring up ideas and have them disregarded at the moment, just to be repeated back as 'new', 3 weeks later. I remember countless moments of being overlooked, shut down, or talked at beyond belief.

Having another woman on the team to vent with was a lifesaver—and working for something I really believed in that got me through." ⁂

"I'm a cis, straight, white man, so no, I don't feel as though I ever was. If people ever had an issue with me, voters specifically, I knew it was always because I was a Democrat and nothing else. I will say though that a lot of my coworkers and people I met on other campaigns that don't share my identity absolutely had a much harder time than I did purely because of what they looked like and other things out of their control." ⁂

"I was fortunate enough not to experience this." ⁂

"In campaign organizing, being talked down to or told you aren't doing your job correctly by volunteers is par for the course for young staffers—especially those identifying as women.

This happened a lot, especially remotely. I think folks feel more comfortable being rude or aggressive when they don't have to talk to someone face-to-face. We had a group chat with all the folks that identified as women on my team, and where we talked through the tough instances." ⁂

"I was treated as an equal member of the team and I felt happy with the group I worked with." ⁂

"No. I feel I was treated extremely well, and enjoyed the opportunity to contribute to the campaign. Being a young person probably presented the starkest difference, and that was more a difference of ideas." ⁂

"In our team in Iowa, we struggled with racial tension and micro-aggressions towards the POC. POC staffers were held to a different standard, and there was a clear divide. I sought comfort in therapy and my fellow POC co-workers." ⁂

"my coworkers and people that *didn't* share my identity *absolutely* had a much harder time than I did"

"I had people on my team that got me confused with the other *non-white* coworkers—even though I had been there for 5-6 months. It could be earnest mistakes but feels weird when it happens repeatedly.

There were also multiple incidents while working with my Georgia runoff team that felt uncomfortable as a poc and women.

For instance, I had to tell the team they couldn't put up a free mural they found on Instagram that had the *'I AM MAN'* signs but instead the signs read *'I AM A VOTE'*. The mural was created by a white guy in Atlanta that just wanted to have a mural up, so he was *'giving'* away the *'art'* he created.

It literally went through every level of approvals, all signing off *'okay'* to put in a gentrified area of Atlanta. I was just 'cc on an email to pull some of our logos to add to the 'free' mural.

The leadership was primarily white (*and not local to Georgia*), but I thought that they would understand how that could make poc feel. It was super hard to say anything. Everyone was so excited that we were going to have a mural up. I texted my friends from the other campaigns I had been on for validation that it felt wrong. I remember shaking, typing the email saying that 'I wasn't comfortable with our team supporting this messaging'. It is weird how many people are given power on a campaign even if they don't understand the demographic or are sensitive to how things can sound to other people.

While the mural didn't go up, it was different after saying something and *not* having anyone say *'oops, our bad—thank you'*. It felt like the people on the email never forgave me or thought of me different after." ∴

"I was sexually harassed by three volunteers and one employee due to my gender. These were always older men, and I heard multiple reports of them being even more disparaging towards the Black women I worked with. One called me a child repeatedly, one implied he'd ask me out if I was old enough (I was 18, he was more than twice that), and one repeatedly noted that despite my age, I was actually pretty competent and "pretty cute too."

I didn't have the time or energy to do much with these issues. One of these volunteers made hundreds of calls a day, and I felt pressured to deal with his demeaning behavior so that he would continue to volunteer with us. I ranted to my friends about it, mentioned it to my female coworkers, and let it be." ∴

"No. As a white woman I live an *extremely* privileged life."

"No mistreatment on my end. Everyone seemed to understand where everyone was coming from a gender/race/sexuality/age standpoint and understood that we could learn from our differences." ∴

"I don't think I had any major negative experiences as a result of my identity. I sometimes experienced rude Zoom comments, a little bit of mansplaining, etc. I am a cis straight able-bodied white woman, which is an identity that I think is really, really privileged in campaign culture." ∴

"I didn't have the *time* or *energy* to do much with these issues."

Question 9

Did you experience *burnout* and how did you cope with it?

"Being virtual was really hard. Our team attempted to do a virtual hangout session, but everyone ended up being too busy—something that did not happen when on an in-person campaign. The work-life balance is harmful to internal campaign culture when virtual.

My role on the campaign depended on me being creative in coming up with and executing ideas. However, especially during holidays, it was hard to feel motivated." ⁂

"At times, I think so. There's no good way to manage it. I just focused on taking care of myself, getting rest the best I could, and taking a break when I could. I can't say I felt at peace until the election was over." ⁂

"I experience burnout, but I also found that in-between campaigns, I was bad at being unemployed. It's hard going from a job that often requires 12-hour workdays, 7 days a week, to having nothing to do.

So much is expected of organizers because the work is incredibly important, but it makes the "self-care" talk feel a little empty. We're told that it's a privilege to work on these campaigns and to be able to make a difference, but we're also told to set boundaries and take care of ourselves.

My bosses were very good at telling me to log off and not answer calls/emails after I signed out for the day, but when your entire role is based on forming relationships with volunteers, it's hard to follow that advice." ⁂

"I did not, but I also did not work full time for the entire duration of the campaign. Burnout did set in with excessive zoom or phone call meetings though because face-to-face interaction is much more engaging and entertaining." ⁂

"At times, I think so. There's no good way to manage it. I just focused on taking care of myself, getting rest the best I could, and taking a break when I could. I can't say I felt at peace until the election was over." ⁂

"Yes, but this was not solely the fault of the campaign. I was working a lot of hours, applying to college, applying for scholarships, and taking classes. Doing both was a lot, and it was very stressful. I started the campaign unpaid and was becoming hesitant about my involvement—I didn't want to work free. Thankfully, I eventually became paid staff.

Not only was this my first campaign job, but it was also my first job—I didn't have a plan to deal with burnout. I did not cope during the cycle with it; I just got through it and took it easy for two weeks after the election." ⁂

"Yes, there were definitely times on the Kamala campaign where I was feeling burnt out. I advocated for self-care and work-life balance more vocally and actively than many campaign staffers. I would leave the office earlier in the evening or request a half-day or a day off more frequently than some of my peers—and I still hit my goals! I do better work when I am well rested and taking care of myself, so I have no problem saying I need the rest." ⁂

"Plenty. Working on a campaign during the 24-hour news cycle was an exhausting experience. To be honest, I didn't have the healthiest coping mechanisms. Fast food and alcohol were a regular part of the routine. Those easy stress relievers feel good at the moment, but they add up in the long run. After the campaign ended, I cut back on both things, which immensely helped.

One healthy coping mechanism I had was running. I ran 5 miles about 4 times a week, and I loved it. Being able to forget everything and grind was a great feeling, and that natural high often carried me through my day. I also tried to spend my time off work doing things other than watching the news. Sports coming back was huge, and it was great to be able to clock out and be invested in something that was low stakes enough that it could be considered a diversion." ⁂

"Campaigns are hard and grueling. This was my first campaign as a paid staffer. It felt like sometimes (due to the pandemic), we had all the not-so-great parts of being on a campaign without the typical camaraderie. We didn't get to spend late nights in field offices or celebrate together after a long hard day/week—these parts would make the tough days easier. My team did the best we could. We had a few PowerPoint parties for team bonding, and they were so fun!" ⁂

"Yes. I probably didn't deal with it very well. I talked to my Co-Field Organizers to try and catch some of their energy, then I told my Regional Director, who made some suggestions. I tried listening to music to pump myself up. I don't think any of those things helped fix the feeling of burnout, though they all likely helped ensure my burnout didn't worsen. From what I remember, my burnout 'fixed' itself after treating my day off as a day off. When GOTV started, there were no more days off. I just didn't have time to be burned out." ⁂

$Q9$ / *Did you experience burnout — how did you cope with it?*

"Yes, I absolutely felt burnout. I worked for roughly 3 months at 40 hours a week, then 3 months at 60-70 hours a week, and a little over 1 month at 90 hours a week. I had about 1 month off and started another month working 70 hours a week.

I was always exhausted, and it hurt my personal relationships. I coped by taking a full day off (including putting my phone 100% out of sight or getting out of service for a long hike) every couple of weeks and trying to get out regularly for walks.

As the nature of all campaigns, I knew it would be temporary, and the desire to win and a new adventure every day kept me pushing through." ⁑

"Definitely. I tried coping in many ways, but I think just developing good friendships with those on our campaign and spending a lot of time with them allowed me to see I wasn't alone in the burnout. Working with them or in new locations also helped. It truly is such demanding emotional work, and I don't really feel like anyone didn't experience burnout." ⁑

"I definitely experienced burnout during my time on campaigns. I turned off all phone notifications after hours and did not respond to any messages after a certain time. After this cycle, I do not think I will ever return to organizing." ⁑

"I was in the burnout zone at times, especially close to the election, but knowing that it would be over soon and under- standing the stakes kept me engaged." ⁑

"I experienced burnout briefly after the November general election post-ballot cure but quickly got back into Senate runoff organizing in Georgia. I experienced burnout in January but quickly got back into state legislature advocacy. My burnout manifests in disillusionment, so I prefer to stay busy to feel impactful and avoid existential depression-esque feelings. I had finals directly following the November election, so I had little time to rest and recover— in fact, I still haven't and don't know when I will (maybe this summer?). I coped by staying afloat, running long-distance, and sleeping a lot." ⁑

"Yes. I am still dealing with the effects of burnout. As much as I am grateful for some incredible experiences, the toll the role took made me deeply sad for quite some time.

Having dealt with serious trauma in my life, it felt wrong to acknowledge that certain experiences led me to that same feeling of trauma for something as 'small' as a job—especially for someone I am happy to have worked for and for values I support.

The one action I took was to support managers for a rotating day off and *real* half-hour lunches/breaks. We needed the room to be humans, to have dignity with our labor. I'm glad I spoke up and advocated for that. I am grateful it was well-received by leadership." ⁑

"Yes. I have come to believe burnout comes with the territory of campaigns. During the campaign, I felt like I was floating on an adrenaline rush that, thank goodness, didn't end until after election day. Our team built each other up, and supported self-care, and I believe that is a big reason I could keep up my energy level during the campaign. Afterward was a different story.

My burnout didn't happen during the campaign but after the cycle. I feel like I'm sandbagging and dragging my feet from day-to-day. I want to do another campaign, but I'm unsure I can yet. My physical energy levels don't match my mental energy levels." ⁂

"Burnout comes *with* the territory of campaigns.

My burnout didn't happen during the campaign but *after* the cycle."

Q9 / *Did you experience burnout — how did you cope with it?*

"Who didn't experience burnout, right!? I struggled a lot toward the end of the campaign, especially in October when we didn't have any days off. I coped with burnout by shutting off my computer when I had a chance, being away from my computer when eating meals, playing a lot of video games, and watching Netflix when I got a couple of free minutes.

I really leaned on my parents for support, I was lucky to be living with them while I worked on the campaign, and they helped by ensuring I had everything I needed. I took my dog on a 20-minute walk every day just to get some fresh air and clear my brain. I realized the campaign would not crash if I was unavailable for 20 minutes, everything would be sitting there waiting for me after my walk." ⁂

"A little bit, I only joined the campaign during the summer, so I didn't face the same two-year marathon that other staffers did. My boss was excellent at making sure we didn't get too burned out." ⁂

"I'm burnt out just thinking about campaigns again! Personally, I maintained relatively healthy boundaries around eating, sleeping, and time off on Team Warren. My direct supervisor was very understanding & understood when I needed to say "no <3." I don't think there was a way to be more grounded on a personal level—I was fully committed to a Warren presidency & the lack of opportunity to heal after dropping out was shattering." ⁂

"In October, the campaign's final month, it was impossible not to feel burnt out. With zero days off for the entirety of the month, it was a win-or-go-home mindset. During this time, it was even more important to lean on the other members of my region on the campaign. Going through the same experience, all chasing a common goal, was a special feeling and experience, and the companionship of my fellow organizers helped push us all through the finish line." ⁂

"Yes. I coped with the burnout in an unhealthy manner; I cried every night after clocking out. I shut out my friends and family and only confided in my boyfriend and mom about the fatigue I was experiencing. I began drinking every evening to take the edge off. It got to the point where I was experiencing a version of Stockholm Syndrome because I had extreme anxiety about being awake and doing anything about the campaign. I refused to quit despite resenting what I was doing. I slept and became extremely depressed for about 2 months after the campaign while mentally healing from the burnout and unhealthy coping strategies I'd adopted." ⁂

"I didn't face the same *two-year* marathon that some other staffers did."

"I absolutely experienced burnout during the cycle. The 2020 cycle led me to have four jobs in one year, move cities three times, and navigate high-intensity jobs without the ability to celebrate wins together in person. To be honest, I think I'm still learning how to cope with it.

What's helped me the most so far has been to try to take as much pressure off my current situation as possible. That can look like muting "personal news!" on Twitter, taking a break from social media entirely, or trying to remind yourself that everyone is on their own journey. Your next job doesn't need to be some perfect, splashy dream job—you're allowed to take whatever work you think would fit your needs for that moment without it being some "step down" from your previous role!

It can also be refreshing to talk to friends outside of the political sphere too—they might think anything you do in politics is cool and respect your efforts to get involved!" ⁂

"PTP did a great job of making sure no one worked more than 45 hours a week, so I didn't experience burnout in that regard. But damn, talking to random people on the phone for 20 hours a week can take a mental toll. I had people threaten my life, call me a bitch, a baby killer, among plenty of other nasty things. There is such an air of almost dismissiveness to these kinds of comments because we are supposed to be "hardened" or whatever, but that shit hurts day in and day out. There was no reprieve from having someone being absolutely disgusting to you. It got to be a bit too much sometimes." ⁂

"It was a rollercoaster of *emotions* working daily as a part of a team fighting for the presidency."

"Yes. It was a rollercoaster of emotions working daily as a part of a team fighting for the presidency. Being around the same people every day would eventually burn me out. When I started getting irritated with people, I would take a work-from-home day to get some space. My job could be very monotonous, leading to burnout at times, but I just reminded myself the campaign doesn't last forever." ⁂

"Absolutely. What got me through my time organizing in Iowa was spending almost every day after work with people I liked relaxing. Whether that's going to a bar or staying in with someone watching tv and eating ice cream, finding something I enjoyed every day kept me sane and helped me break out of the stress of campaign work." ⁂

"I experienced intense burnout and coped with it by going to therapy and talking with some co-field organizers with whom I felt comfortable sharing. I barely coped and *am* still recovering from burnout almost 4 months later." ⁂

"It's hard to know what to do next. It's hard to feel like you were *running* a marathon nonstop & boom, everything ends. Your friendships, routines, the chaos—"

"Yes, I did. This was the first job that had demanded more than 40hrs a week for me. I just came from university and was used to late nights and early mornings. I coped with the long days by making friends in the office. I had a solid group of friends within the Operations Team (and I still talk to them today!). We would make each other take 15-minute walk breaks outside to make sure we got some sunshine. We would pick up coffee or lunch for each other too. Since none of us worked directly under each other, we could share our frustrations with our bosses when they came up.

I also made sure to take care of myself outside of the office. This was my first time being in Boston, and I knew I wouldn't live there forever, so I took every opportunity I had to explore this new, exciting city. I also was lucky to have a manager who under-stood the importance of mental health and community. Every Tuesday, I was unavailable for one hour to attend therapy; every Friday, I was unavailable for two hours to attend a Shabbat service." ⁎

"A little, I think. Truthfully, I may be experi-encing it now. It's hard to know what to do next. It's hard to feel like you were running a marathon nonstop & then boom, every-thing ends. Your friendships, routines, the chaos—it's a really weird feeling. It felt like it ended so suddenly—we had an end date, we knew when Election Day was, but I wasn't mentally prepared for how friendships would fade and how losing a race could make you feel tiny & like you sacrificed a TON for nothing. I turned to build new routines, giving myself reasons to get out of bed, chores, walks, writing reviews on my experience in roles I had during the cycle." ⁎

"Yes. Working 65–80-hour weeks is very draining. I slept at least 8 hours and drank a lot of hot chocolate from Casey's. It was hard because campaigns preached "self-care," but there was such a toxic overachiever presence on campaign Twitter. It was an exhausting [experience]." ⁎

"Absolutely. There are no real hours on campaigns. You develop a "campaign brain" to the point that you find yourself replying to emails at midnight. Work-life balance is virtually non-existent. When doing what you feel is such important work, it is hard not to throw yourself into it completely. This was something I enjoyed and would do again, despite the occasional burnout, but I would not be able to do it forever. Coping by going to social events like happy hours after work was fun early on, but during COVID, it was much harder to unplug." ⁎

"I definitely experienced burnout by the end of the campaign. I didn't cope with it. But watching Harry Potter helped." ⁎

"I did. My turf was the most Republican in the district, and it was hard to recruit volunteers. Honestly, what I did was just let everything else go; stopped working out, stopped studying for the LSAT and just kind of used all of my time off to rest and recharge." ⁎

"Yes! Some burnout from work, but a lot of exhaustion and stress from the pandemic. I tried to incorporate rest and social time into my routine as much as possible, which helped. I am grateful to have a lot of friends and family who know nothing about campaigns, and spending time with them feels relaxing and a bit like leaving the campaign bubble. Also, over the course of the cycle, I transitioned into higher-level roles that I found more fulfilling. I experi-enced less burnout in these new roles, even though I was working way more hours." ⁎

Question 10

What *boundaries* and routines do you recommend young campaign *staffers* to put in place for self-care?

"Communication is key. If you are open with your manager about how you need time to step away or decompress, they can help you and your workload." ⁂

"Please always take your days off. They are not for work. Once you leave the office, do not work. I left my laptop at the office most days. Please treasure the time you have off because it is a precious commodity." ⁂

"I'd say to ask questions about what's expected of you and to make sure that you're told what your schedule is going to be, especially as you get closer to GOTV. It's okay to work hard for things that you care about, but you'll do that best if you are able to follow a schedule." ⁂

"Set firmer hours. Try not to be working on the campaign at all hours of the night. Specialize, instead of being a jack of all trades like I was. Be honest about what you are prepared to contribute, and be realistic about the challenges of the race you are in. If you can, don't be afraid to walk away from a campaign that is mistreating you." ⁂

"Set time aside for yourself, despite whether or not your friends on the campaign want to hang out after work. Enjoy some peace and quiet by yourself, and read a book!" ⁂

"I think a lot of this comes from effective management. I hate to put all of it on young people to, like, take a bath when really it should come from their superiors setting healthy boundaries and expectations around work. But, as organizer memes say, drink your water and get some sleep." ⁂

"Take small breaks during the day, spend some time outside, exercise, hydrate, eat well, and get enough sleep. Whatever you're doing on a campaign, the team needs your creativity and presence of mind, and you will only be able to do your best work if you're taking care of yourself. Others may cope better, but sacrificing my wellbeing for work is not a tradeoff that works out. I may work longer hours, but my creativity completely tanks and the quality of my work suffers tremendously. Staying healthy will keep you happier and produce better work. Finally, if possible, I'd recommend trying to find types of work within your job that require different kinds of thought. Personally, I find that working different parts of my brain keeps my sharper and makes me less likely to burn out. I did this at school too, I tried not to take too many similar classes." ⁂

"To be honest, I did not have a routine, but looking back, I would have done things differently. My classes were all online, so I wish that I would have done all my homework on the weekends and dedicated the week to applying for college, applying for scholarships, and working on the campaign during the week. I also wish I would have stopped at seven each night just so that I had time for myself at night." ⁂

"Don't put so much pressure on yourself! While it may feel like the weight of the world is on your shoulders, at the end of the day it is the job of the candidate to get the votes needed to win. Give your all, but never accept personal blame when your candidate doesn't come out on top." ⁂

"Unionize & develop relationships with union leadership before crisis hits. You do not have to work where you do not have support or understanding. Always eat food every day, stay hydrated, and listen to your body. Be aware of the scarcity mindset of campaigning & encourage yourself to put your needs [as a] higher priority." ⁂

"ask questions about what's expected of you and make sure you're told what your schedule is going to be."

"Setting strict office and work hours! My boss gave me this advice when I was hired and I'll repeat it for as long as I work on campaigns. Setting these guidelines from the beginning sets the precedent that that is your time, and you will take care of whatever issue there is tomorrow if someone is trying to contact you after your work hours.

Step away. Whether it be from the office, your screen, or from a phonebank to grab a snack, just step away every so often. Take a walk, grab a coffee, and don't forget to exercise and eat. It's so easy to forget self-care during a campaign because their cause we're fighting for is so great, but we need to take care of ourselves too. And don't feel guilty for taking that time for yourself!

Trust your coworkers and your volunteers. If you have done your job correctly everyone knows what they're doing by GOTV; don't stress yourself trying to do everything for everyone. Assign and train for roles, set clear expectations, and let everyone do their job well. By the end of our campaign I had volunteers running entire phone banks and I didn't even need to be on the Zoom, and as someone who likes control this was tough for me, but I knew that I had provided them with every resource they needed to be successful, and that I trusted them enough to run events without me there. The beauty of this is that many of these volunteers went on to become strong community leaders even after the campaigns." ⁂

Q10 / *What boundaries and routines do you recommend young campaign staffers to put in place for self-care?*

"Days off!!!!!!!!!!!!!!!!!!!!!!!!! Rotating days off so some organizers are working everyday can work FINE. Working organizers, deputies, regionals, etc. into the ground and having it be so normal is completely in contrast for many of the progressive policies and values we preach to uphold. Self care tips and self care articles mean nothing if we aren't creating the space for folks to rest and recharge. Overworking should not be a normalized symbol of success." ⁂

"In a normal, non-pandemic world, I'd say take some work from home days. Get your chores done and relax on those days. Also I made sure to take the time every morning to get dressed and put makeup on. It was a very nice relaxing 20 minutes of my morning just to myself, and made me feel good all day, and at night I always took 10 minutes of peace to do my skincare routine.

The main boundary I wish I put up was: it's okay to take time off for family. This is kind of a personal problem stemming from toxic work (and sport) environments in high school and college. I always feel like if I step away from my work, I'll fall soooo far behind and lose my job or status and experience FOMO. This led me to not taking any time off while on the campaign to go visit my dying aunt. But part of that was also a coping mechanism, and I took time off for the funeral and a wedding. If your colleagues are good people they will know family should come first and it's okay to take time off. If they don't understand this then they are simply bad people and you shouldn't work with them." ⁂

"In October, the campaign's final month, it was impossible not to feel burnt out. With zero days off for the entirety of the month, it was a win-or-go-home mindset. During this time, it was even more important to lean on the other members of my region on the campaign. Going through the same experience, all chasing a common goal, was a special feeling and experience, and the companionship of my fellow organizers helped push us all through the finish line." ⁂

"Yes. I coped with the burnout in an unhealthy manner; I cried every night after clocking out. I shut out my friends and family and only confided in my boyfriend and mom about the fatigue I was experiencing. I began drinking every evening to take the edge off. It got to the point where I was experiencing a version of Stockholm Syndrome because I had extreme anxiety about being awake and doing anything about the campaign. I refused to quit despite resenting what I was doing. I slept and became extremely depressed for about 2 months after the campaign while mentally healing from the burnout and unhealthy coping strategies I'd adopted." ⁂

"Check in with your family and friends outside of the campaign to remind yourself of the outside world, try to make time to cook meals instead of eating out or ordering in, and try to walk to work or stay active in a way that easily fits into your campaign schedule." ⁂

"No one will ever care about you more than you.

You can't expect your boss or anyone to *prioritize* your well-being above the work at hand."

"No one will ever care about you more than you. You can't expect your boss or anyone else to prioritize your well-being above the work at hand. That's why it's so important to constantly be listening to your body and your needs so that you can be at your best.

I feel like I hear the same things from everyone, but there are a few essentials that have worked for me. I think the big recommendations I have would be to drink as much water as you can, maintain some type of interest outside of campaigns/politics, keep a to-do list, and do at least one thing for yourself every day. Water is pretty obvious, but speaking from experience, it is simply not sustainable to live off of iced coffee/pop/energy drinks.

I know campaign work pretty much takes up all of your personal bandwidth, especially in the closing days, however I think it's important you do your best to maintain relationships and interests outside of campaigns because otherwise it becomes so much easier to burn out.

The most important thing that has gotten me through every job I've had is to keep a to-do list. There is always so much to do, but when you keep a list of the essentials or most important things that you can focus on, I feel like it keeps your day focused and intentional. And whether it's a 30-minute walk, a little bit of Mario Kart, or however you relax best, I have found that if you can do one small thing for yourself every day, the day seems to go better." ✶

"Unionize! Really stop working when you stop working. Ask for help. Try to get comfortable with polite rejections in order to avoid spreading yourself too thin. Go to therapy!" ✶

"Work for the Jaime Harrison digital team where your boss Bailey Stonecipher will do an incredible job making sure everyone gets their work done but never feels too stressed or burnt out. Also make sure you exercise, eat right, and don't go to bed at 2 AM each night." ✶

$Q10$ / *What boundaries and routines do you recommend young campaign staffers to put in place for self-care?*

"Get at least 8 hours of sleep. Call your family/a loved one often to remind yourself that there's more to life than work. Don't go on twitter on days off/after work hours. Spend time by yourself. And unionize. Campaigns don't need to be 12 hours, 6 days a week for minimum wage. Our campaigns are LOADED and are overpaying consultants." ⁂

"Boundaries and routines should be prescribed by upper-level staff. Democratic campaigns should live up to the values they preach. Better hours, better pay, and strict boundaries are necessary. It's unfair to ask young campaign staffers to set these boundaries because they may hurt their future networking chances if they do not jump when they're asked to. The organizing world seems to favor people with connections over people with talent.

I recommend that young staffers turn off their phone and email notifications after a certain time. Days off should be spent not thinking about work. Unionize where possible. Schedule out your day in advance and manage your time well. Ask for help when you need it." ⁂

"Democratic campaigns should live up to the values they preach."

"I love having parts of my life that have literally nothing to do with electoral politics—like I love reading fashion magazines. I also find it really fulfilling and fueling to be part of movement-building work that is separate from electoral politics. I also try really, really hard to stay connected with my friends. I would encourage young staffers to think about community care in addition to self-care: how can you be part of your community? what can you give your community? How can you ask for your community to support you?" ⁂

"Close your computer at lunch and when you sign off your checkout call. Give yourself a few minutes between closing your last Zoom and opening Netflix on your computer. Especially if you are still organizing digitally the mental strain of staring at a computer all day is tough. People were honestly talking about drinking enough water, but my bigger issue was remembering to eat or carving out time to eat during the day. Remember that the campaign is not going to come to a screeching halt if you get up and take a walk for 20 minutes, sure there are plenty of people counting on you but do not ever take the position that the whole country is counting on you hitting your call goal for the day or that the campaign might lose if you don't hit call goal." ⁂

"It is important to hold yourself to a hard stop on the time that you stop doing work things. You cannot be good at your job if you're not eating, sleeping, and going outside once in a while. Also if you do not do this before dry runs start, you will never do it!

Organizers, break up call time. It is not feasible or sustainable to consistently make 100 dials in one sitting without a break or getting some water." ⁂

"WOW! Self-care is hard, it's something I struggle with & boundaries will be your best friend but may feel incredibly uncomfortable to set. Honestly, please pay attention to your body! (Physically, mentally, emotionally) You matter! Every election is important but there is not another you! Please pay attention to your feelings & experiences even when no one else is. That being said if you need to, go to the doctor! I ended up in Emergency Surgery near the end of September 2020 and back to work within 24 hours; it's not something I am proud of. I needed to heal. I deserved to heal but instead I was afraid of setting boundaries/saying "no."

My saving grace was changing my phone settings so that my phone would light up but not ring or vibrate without using do not disturb. This allowed me to put my phone down without being interrupted and without being called out for having my phone on do not disturb/sending people directly to voicemail.

Put blocks on your Google Calendar that look normal to fellow campaign staffers/bosses perhaps label an hour block as "1:1 with XX" then use that 1-hour block to go to therapy! Do whatever you need to to not feel embarrassed about therapy/self-care. Your work will get done, don't sacrifice taking care of yourself." ⁂

"A really important boundary for me was finding some place that I could be fully offline, even for just 30 minutes. I was lucky enough to spend most of this cycle in Los Angeles, and for me going in the ocean with no phone, watch, or laptop provided a really necessary moment of peace. I also made the decision not to work while I ate meals! I think campaign life mixed with work from home can become toxic when you're expected to be available every second of the day. For me, taking 20-30 minutes to eat breakfast, lunch, or dinner without working was really important to stay sane." ⁂

"I recommend not working overtime just because you feel pressured to, or because someone tells you you are important and your extra effort would be valued. I recommend being honest with your friends and family about your workload and stress so they can adequately support you. I recommend prioritizing sleep and the simplest, easiest forms of self care like petting your dog daily or making sure you have time to eat three meals if possible." ⁂

"I wish I could scream "You are not your labor! Your labor is not your worth!" to anyone entering these spaces for the first time. I think I'd tell folks to advocate for themselves and to engage in some serious labor organizing for their fellow campaign workers. I want to see a HQ presidential campaign staff finally be a part of a collective bargaining agreement. I want to see folks care less about their 'ownership' of projects they'll forget about in a week and more about the struggle of their fellow workers. I'd advise that part of looking after yourself means looking after others. The truth is, this culture survives because certain individuals thrive on it—frequently those without children, without disabilities, without significant obligations at home. My advice is to establish boundaries with yourself and to constantly vocalize those boundaries, to do all you can to have them respected. On a practical level, to take a lunch break, to schedule therapy and doctor's appointments. To allow yourself more kindness than is shown to you by others." ⁂

"You are *not* your labor! Your labor is not your *worth*!"

"Not everything in the world *revolves* around politics, but it's hard to see that from *inside* the campaign bubble."

"I would recommend making your boundaries known as early as possible. When I first started my full-time position I told my manager that I would need time off every week for therapy and church. We were able to agree on clear expectations and boundaries because I made my needs known at the beginning of our work together.

Know who is on the HR team and how to contact them. Do not be afraid to reach out with any concerns or complaints you might have. That is why they are there!

It's great to make friends on the campaign because they will understand exactly what you are going through, but it's also helpful to keep in touch with your non-political friends. When the work felt overwhelming and I was discouraged in our progress I could always call my school friends who would tell me about their engineering class or their new puppy. Not everything in the world revolves around politics, but it's hard to see that from inside the campaign bubble." ⁂

"If you're lucky enough to get a day off, actually take it off! And unionize if possible." ⁂

"Unionize early and set really strict standards for the workplace. The campaign will start to push back and "give you opportunities" to work more hours than your union contract states, which is a great way to earn more money, but don't allow it to become an expectation. Campaigns have obscene amounts of money and can afford to hire an extra person to avoid burning you out, even though they don't want to. It is NOT normal to work 45+ hours a week for a paycheck that breaks down to below minimum wage per hour. It is NOT normal to feel anxious that you aren't "doing enough" because you worked your union-required hour-maximum and didn't exploit yourself for the campaign. And it is NOT normal to be required to be available via phone/video call 24/7. Set boundaries early and don't be afraid to enforce them when they aren't being respected. It's hard to do at first because many of us join politics to change the world and feel that you should give it all your effort, but you shouldn't sacrifice your wellbeing when the campaign has the resources to alleviate the pressure on you." ⁂

"Don't allow campaigns to take advantage of you because of your inexperience and need for work. Part of the campaign culture is about feeling like you are truly a part of something bigger and more important than just your work, but campaigns can abuse that to have you work yourself to burnout. Join a campaign where your own mental health is actually valued by giving you days off and setting clear work/life boundaries." ⁂

"Work hard during the workday and stop when work is over. Once or twice a week, if you're feeling swamped during the day, either stay late or start early and clear out your email/do that one task you need to do. I despise working outside the required hours because that way lies madness, but I also know that you're going to have way too much work to do, and if you can prevent future you from feeling overwhelmed, future you will thank you very very much.

I also put my phone on Do Not Disturb between 10pm and 7am.

I always tried to take ~15 minutes before the workday started to listen to a (non politics) podcast or music, or just relax. Getting my head out of the politics headspace makes me remember that while it feels like the future of our country depends on you, and sometimes your RODs/other managers will be toxic and make you think that, and it's important to remember that isn't true. You're still just a person.

Our campaign also put in place a "sustainabilibuddies" thing that mostly didn't amount to much, but it took staffers (all of the same seniority-level) and paired them up with someone from either a different region or a different department, and the only thing we did was, like, check in on each other and share pictures of animals." ⁂

"I found it really hard to say *no* to anything, and while that always brought some kind of new experience, it definitely *hurt* over time."

Q10 / *What boundaries and routines do you recommend young campaign staffers to put in place for self-care?*

"Be diligent about what your coping mechanisms are and whether or not they're healthy in the long run. Also, keep a healthy distance from the news cycle. Obviously staying informed is good, but there's a point to which you become locked into the political news cycle and it consumes you. Get hobbies. Get invested in things that are apolitical. Try to talk to friends about stuff that isn't the campaign. Keep a healthy distance between yourself and your work. It's sometimes seen as noble to be so fully invested in a campaign that it becomes a core part of your personality, but there's a reason that burnout rates and cynicism in this field are so high. Put your physical and mental health first and the rest of your priorities will be better off for it." ⁖

"I found that having check-ins with some of my fellow organizers was very helpful; we'd ask each other if we had eaten and stayed hydrated throughout the day. It's so easy to get too caught up in your work, especially if the day or week demands it as you near Election Day, so I think having that support system from your team members is great. Additionally, I would say to set aside certain hours where you don't focus on anything work related. This may sound obvious, like normally one would dismiss work-related correspondence once they were getting ready for bed, but in our field, it feels like you work around the clock. It wasn't uncommon for me to work through meals or just skip eating entirely, or check emails even if it was well into the night, or try and absorb all the news articles I couldn't get to earlier in my workday. It really affects your personal life and relationships, so finding that work-life balance as early as you can will benefit you in the long run. ⁖

"I kept a journal where I logged the amount of water I was drinking, the meals I was eating, the amount of sleep I was getting, and what I planned to do to take care of myself that week. It helped me hold myself accountable and kept me from slipping in terms of self-care. I also would just say don't be scared to advocate for yourself. An environment where advocating for yourself and your self-care causes retribution or pushback from your manager(s) is not one you want to be in anyway." ⁖

"It is important to hold yourself to a hard stop on the time that you stop doing work things. You cannot be good at your job if you're not eating, sleeping, and going outside once in a while. Also if you do not do this before dry runs start, you will never do it!
Organizers, break up call time. It is not feasible or sustainable to consistently make 100 dials in one sitting without a break or getting some water." ⁖

"Guaranteed time off. We were all working 7 days a week during the last month of the campaign and it was awful. I need to know that I'll be able to take a day to myself without needing to be on my deathbed for it to be cleared." ⁖

"I needed to *know* that I'll be able to take a *day* to myself without needing to be on my deathbed for it to be cleared."

"[campaign life] really affects your personal life an relationships, so finding that work–life balance as *early* as you can will benefit you in the long run."

Question 11

How did your position(s) on this cycle fit into your career goals?

"While I do not want to pursue further roles in field, my positions this cycle helped me realize that. My positions as an FO and a coach helped me understand what I like and what I don't like about working in politics, and have led to a narrower focus for jobs I am looking to next. I feel that all of my positions helped me develop incredibly valuable skills for future jobs even though I want to leave field." ⁂

"I had planned on going into entertainment, but after such an excellent experience I've decided to stay in politics for the near future." ⁂

"None of my positions directly fit into my career goals. With that being said, I grew as a person during this campaign. I do not enjoy talking to people, and this expanded my horizons. I became more confident talking to people as the campaign went on. I will surely use this in any career field I end up working in." ⁂

"I found my experience in this cycle to be incredibly foundational. Although some of it likely won't be applicable in the future once COVID-19 is a memory, getting the experience of reaching out to voters, even in a hostile field, and working for ideas that I believe in was very enjoyable and greatly appreciated. As I prepare to go to law school, and consider what kind of future I might have in politics, I feel that being on the ground in a sense was valuable to my knowledge and growth." ⁂

"It didn't necessarily; I just wanted to help out my community" ⁂

"I'm not really sure. I wanted to try out campaign life and make a contribution. I suspect this experience will be important, I'm just not sure exactly where it fits into my story at this point." ⁂

"I want to work in the policy field, and I was working on a policy-based campaign." ⁂

"I want to work on a legislative team, and I think field organizing helped because talking about policy with people who generally were hearing about that policy for the first time brought some interesting viewpoints, some of which I hadn't previously considered. The average person holds a relatively idiosyncratic belief system and is mostly uninvolved in politics. That's very different from your average organizer. Hearing takes that forced me to defend the policy I was advocating for was good because it deepened my understanding of the legislation itself. It's like how you can understand a class better by teaching the material to a friend or colleague that isn't taking the course. Explaining and debating political ideas to people who aren't familiar with them gives me a stronger knowledge of those ideas, and that's a practice I want to take with me in my career as a policy professional." ⁂

"In college when I thought about jobs, I always figured 'okay when I graduate in 2020 I literally have to be a part of a campaign that cycle because I will simply lose my mind if I'm not a part of that. After that I'll go from there.' I think it's hard to develop career goals." ⁂

"My position as a field organizer opened me up to a bunch of great connections for my career goals, but it also affirmed for me that I didn't want to work in politics again. I love the advocacy and legal sides of campaign work and had used the connections I made during the cycle to launch myself into my current job in law, but being a field organizer just affirmed for me that I never wanted a career in politics." ⁂

"I was able to move from being an organizer, which I loved, into roles where I got to think about strategy and how to build strong organizing programs. I feel more ready to take on strategic planning and program creation in a non-campaign context." ⁂

"I love that I have experience as an organizer and as a data staffer. I have been encouraging everyone I speak to that is interested in political data to start as an organizer so they can carry that perspective into their work later. I am so much better at my job of supporting organizers because I have a sense of what they need. It worked out really nicely that I found a data role that would invest in me as an organizer with no prior data experience and I got to learn a ton of helpful skills including administrative VAN skills, advanced Google Sheets, and coding in SQL. Those are really important skills for higher up data roles and that's where I am hoping to go so my positions set me up really nicely." ⁂

"I do want to work in politics, I loved training and managing volunteers, I'm not sure how it fits with my career goals but I do know that it gave me so many skills that I am able to show off to future employers such as time management, attention to detail, mass communication, and managing people from various backgrounds. I do not think organizing is my final career by any means, I would love to work in state or local government but just the experience of this cycle is something I can be proud of and point to for future employers to look at." ⁂

"I'm not sure! Following the campaign, I immediately started a job in healthcare communications in NYC. I still follow politics with the same passion and interest as before, and hope to reenter the field one day." ⁂

"I am currently applying to law schools. These roles allowed me to work on issues I care about and to get experience in advocacy, which is my ultimate goal." ⁂

"It was almost perfect. I planned on going into politics at the time." ⁂

$Q11$ / *How did your position(s) on this cycle fit into your career goals?*

"I have always dreamed of a career in which I get to work with a variety of individuals, work toward positive/meaningful change for others and so every position I had has allowed me to do just this & along the way I learned I love digital more than traditional field and so far I love training/teaching others the most!" ∴

"I want to work in the field so it allows me to build experience!" ∴

"My career goals have shifted a lot because of the roles I was able to have in this cycle. I started on the Warren campaign in paid media which I loved, but soon realized I didn't want to do forever and wanted to get a more holistic understanding of all the other opportunities the digital space had to offer. With the Democratic National Convention was able to try a lot of things ranging from social media, to some press relationships, digital partnerships, influencer marketing and more. That experience, which I continued at the Biden campaign and inauguration teams, really helped me home in on what I want to do in the future." ∴

"I'd love to work in congressional politics one day. I thought maybe working on campaigns would be a nice stepping stone. It will be. Just lots of negativity right now because of my long-term unemployment." ∴

"I thought it would fit better but after the pandemic, I'm not sure if/how I'll actively tap back into this professional space." ∴

"Honestly I don't know. I'm not sure what my 5-year plan is, or even what my 2-year plan is. I know that this was my first year working on campaigns, and I loved it. I'm just interested to see what I can do in the world of campaigns next." ∴

"To be completely honest, I'm unsure what career trajectory I want. However, I think working on local politics is eventually the goal. Working on digital in a campaign showed me a lot of how different departments fit in and everything that's needed to be successful." ∴

"This position helped fit into my career goals to help train other social workers to run for office and work on campaigns to ensure there are more ethical and sustainable choices made for staff on campaigns" ∴

"I want to work in elections law, downballot organizing, and mutual aid/socialist organizing moving forward, so much of this work was beneficial. I got to work with and meet dozens of amazing downballot candidates and organizers in that ecosystem, and I gained a broad range of experiences in voter protection.

I made invaluable connections with organizers in my state and a reputation for hard work and inspiration. I now have a clearer idea of the good I want to do in the world." ∴

"My position on the congressional campaign gave me experience and helped toward my career goals more than I ever thought it would. It gave me important perspective on how hard it would be to work on campaigns full time every cycle. I am passionate about getting progressives into office and fighting for the issues that matter to me. I think electoral politics is one of the best ways to make a difference there and I'd love to work on campaigns in the future. My experience on both campaigns last year helped me make incredible connections and narrow my interests in a way that I know will serve me well in the future." ∴

"I wanted to continue working in the nonprofit sector, but most of my previous experience has been with a completely different industry altogether. Furthermore, I had been with a nonprofit organization whose work was more globally minded and focused on diplomacy, so I wanted experience with a political organization where I could work more closely with local communities.

My role as a digital organizer was my first, full-time paid political position, as well as my first time working during an election cycle. I was exposed to a lot of new learning experiences regarding legislation and advocacy, something that I feel would not have happened otherwise if I did not seek out the role. Moving forward, I want to continue working with the nonprofit sector within the next couple of years, and would enjoy it if the organization has some involvement with my state's legislative session or specific advocacy projects." ⁂

"It was good to get the hands-on experience and skills that comes from the field, but I learned I never want to do field [work] again." ⁂

"Because I was on the Operations Team, I have been able to be nuanced in my career so far. I am currently working as the Operations Manager of an anti-racism consulting firm. While it is not exactly political work, I could not have gotten this job without the experience and knowledge I gained on the Warren team." ⁂

"I didn't pursue the FO position because of career plans. I genuinely just needed a job and knew I could do it. I want to be involved in advocacy work, though, so the experience managing volunteers and recruiting volunteer leaders is valuable." ⁂

"I'm not sure that I have overly well-defined career goals, however it was a dream come true to have worked on a presidential campaign, especially one that ended up being successful. It was also a dream come true to be a real campaign manager, and the fact that I was able to win a race as a campaign manager was pretty unreal. Given that I was able to accomplish things that I didn't think I would be able to during my first cycle, I've had to reevaluate my career goals." ⁂

"I learned a lot. The skills I gained doing campaign work vastly improved my communication, organizational, and inter-personal skills. I hope to work for the State Department someday, so electing leaders/public servants I believe in matters to me. Seeing the American electoral process up close and firsthand is really special. It's a great foundation for so many different kinds of work." ⁂

"I want to continue working in policy and advocacy, and thought there is no better time to join a movement than post college. I needed to seize the opportunity or I would've regretted it. I have learned so much about politics, about myself and what it means to engage." ⁂

"I want to work in progressive/Democratic politics, so the 2 campaigns definitely helped me gain some experience and meet people. As I mentioned, I found that I don't handle consistent unemployment super well, so I'm hoping to use the campaign experience to do something more long-term, but I have the general goal of getting Democrats elected and enacting progressive policies." ⁂

Question 12

Do you plan on staying in politics?

"I certainly hope so. There's too much work to do. I always told my mother that if we let politics be the realm of the corrupt, only the corrupt will ever dare to try. The challenges at hand require a generation that will rise to the moment. And no one is going to save the world for us. Whether that's helping other candidates or becoming one myself, I hope to do the best I can, however I can." ⁂

"I think one of the most amazing things that came out of this cycle was the people that were able to be a part of this campaign cycle because so many things were being done remote. This brought a lot of folks into campaigns that would not have otherwise been able to be a part of it, and it should by no means be a one-time thing!" ⁂

"Yes, always. I can't imagine finding anything else very interesting." ⁂

"Yes, I would love to stay involved in politics, but I am not sure I would love to work on another campaign in a paid position. When I was filling this survey out, my tax information came, and I had to pay almost as much as my mom did in taxes even though I made substantially less. I do not have a ton of money saved up, and I will be in college soon. I can't afford to have almost 20% taken out for taxes when I am trying not to take out student loans. In addition, the campaign was incredibly draining, and I need to keep up my GPA to get into law school, so I most likely will not be taking an active role in campaigns in the near future. I would love to be a civil rights attorney, and I would also like to hold public office one day myself." ⁂

"Not in the short-term, but I suspect I'll be back." ⁂

"Yes, absolutely. Right now I am looking to intern in a legislative office for the summer, but I definitely hope to work on an election again soon." ⁂

"Yes. I know that I don't have the energy or stamina to do campaigns forever though, and I would like to one day go into advocacy/non-profit work." ⁂

"Yes, but I am still on the fence about continuing with campaigns!" ⁂

"For now, I am happy in my job (they give me weekends off! LOL). Eventually, I think it is my passion and dream to re-enter politics. As a country, I truly believe there is a want to be so much better than we are, and I believe our generation has so much potential to leave the Earth having affected positive change. Remember the name because you haven't seen the last of me yet!" ⁂

"I'm not exactly sure at the moment—I think taking a short break might make sense for me right now but I can't picture myself ever permanently leaving the field." ⁂

"Yes, but maybe not field. Field is tough and honestly kudos to anyone who does that long-term because you are a warrior and a soldier and this country rests on your shoulders." ⁂

"Yes, probably. I'm hoping that the pandemic will make the often toxic and burnout culture in campaigning end. I want to be able to have a work-life balance and campaigning doesn't currently allow for that, even if I'm super passionate about the work." ⁂

"Yes! I never expected to end up in politics but I am so grateful that I did & have already learned & grown so much. I would love to pursue a role in policy/advocacy or tech tools as I do yearn for a position with at least a little work/life balance." ⁂

"Yes, without question." ⁂

"Yes! Although at the moment I don't have a defined path, I love working in the nonprofit sector, and hope that I can experience working with an organization that does outreach and advocacy for youth development or environmental justice." ⁂

"Yes I plan to stay in politics and politically adjacent work. While I am currently doing consulting, I would like to return to the campaign circuit come 2024. I have always had the goal of writing and enacting policy and I am still determined to make that my reality in the future." ⁂

"In a way, yes. I want to work on policy analysis rather than campaigns." ⁂

"In the immediate future I hope to stay in politics, but on the official side as opposed to campaigns. Open to many different opportunities, however. If I find a good fit for me in campaigns, I'll go for it!" ⁂

"I'm unsure but leaning towards no. Although I live in Texas, so if Beto runs for governor, I'm dropping out of college to work on his campaign." ⁂

Appendix

Compensation Breakdown

The dynamic nature of the election cycle and varying budgets can make it challenging for new staffers to advocate for fair pay. More transparency across the board is needed for ensuring fair compensation for future staffers.

Because some roles only exist for less than a year, pay for campaign jobs is typically calculated by month rather than a yearly salary. Some interviewees began working as unpaid interns or hourly employees before transitioning to full-time roles with a monthly salary and benefits.

The lowest reported salary for a full-time employee was $1,500 per month with a U.S. House race. This staffer got a raise later in the cycle, totaling $4,000/month in compensation.

The highest-paying roles were all at the manager or director level for first-time staffers in the 2020 cycle. The highest compensation for first-time staffers reported was $6,250/month from Inauguration Committee, *Biden for President*, and *Democratic National Convention*. The next highest-paying employers were *Tom Steyer 2020* ($6,122/month) and *Jon Ossoff for Senate* ($6,000/month).

Monthly Compensation for First-Time Staffers across 2020
Average pay across multiple roles staffers held throughout the cycle

$1,500
(low)

$3,953
(average)

$6,250
(high)

$3,729
Average among
organizing roles

The most common role for a first-time staffer in 2020 was in an organizing position. Within the organizing, the highest-paying roles for first-time staffers were in the Georgia Senate runoff election and with Mike Bloomberg's campaign, earning $5,700 and $6,000 per month, respectively. The top-paying roles were unique cases due to the short timeframe and national focus of the Georgia runoff election as well as Bloomberg's self-funding.

The average pay for organizers was $3,729 per month in 2020. The compensation for first-time staff in the 2020 election cycle was lower than a report stating that recent graduates in 2020 earned an average of $4,605 per month.[29]

Some campaigns provided their employees healthcare, paid time off, 401(k) plans, and other benefits. Despite often working beyond the standard 40-hour work week, many campaign and election staffers were not eligible for overtime compensation.

Throughout the 2020 cycle, many staffers saw pay increases and promotions as they moved between campaigns. Staffers who remained with primary campaigns that advanced to the general election also received promotions and pay raises as fundraising efforts ramped up and campaigns secured more resources.

Overall, the payment for first-time staffers in the 2020 election varied depending on the scale of the race, individual negotiations, and campaign/organizational pay standards. While campaign work was demanding, it was a source of income and employment for those starting their careers in a tough job market during the Covid-19 pandemic.

29. Herrity, J. (2023, February 16). Average salary in the US (with demographic data). Pay & Salary. https://www.indeed.com/career-advice/pay-salary/average-salary-in-us

Endnotes and Sources

1. Democratic values which many of my ex-classmates who have moved out of state now support.

2. Friend, E., Clark, R., Thibodeau, J., Kent, J. (2020, September 22). *Ed Markey's relational-first organizing approach.* https://medium.com/@emma.h.friend/ed-mar-keys-relational-first-organizing-approach-137bbfc4852

3. Leonard, D., Stein, Z., Kravitz, J. (2022, April 11). *How we built a relational network of 160K voters in less than a month.* https://medium.com/@davisleonard/how-we-built-a-relational-network-of-160k-voters-in-less-than-a-month-92262926fdb0

4. *Campaign manager demographics and statistics [2023]: Number of campaign managers in the US.* Campaign Manager Demographics and Statistics [2023]: Number Of Campaign Managers In The US. (2022, September 9). https://www.zippia.com/campaign-manager-jobs/demographics

5. Bograd, S. (2020, October 28). *Recent college grads are running political campaigns.* Teen Vogue. https://www.teenvogue.com/story/campaign-managers-state-local-elections

6. Democratic Party efforts are being defined as state Democratic Parties and efforts such as 'Texas Democratic Party' and 'Maine Democratic Party Coordinated Campaign.'

7. Organization efforts include any group that is not directly related to a campaign or the Democratic Party but is doing work directly related to voter turnout or the election. Eg. 'One Campaign for Michigan' or *'When We All Vote'*.

8. The Economist Newspaper. (n.d.). *Who is ahead in the Democratic primary race?*. The Economist. https://projects.economist.com/democratic-primaries-2020

9. Kirby , E. H., & Kawashima-Ginsberg, K. (2019, August 17). *The Youth Vote in 2008 .* Youth on the Trail 2012. http://www.whatkidscando.org/youth.on.the.trail.2012/pdf/IOP.Voters.Guide.pdf

10. Dimock, M. (2023, May 11). *Defining generations: Where millennials end and generation Z begins.* Pew Research Center. https://www.pewresearch.org/fact-tank/2019/01/17/where-millennials-end-and-generation-z-begins

11 Whittier, N. (1997). *Political Generations, Micro-Cohorts, and the Transformation of Social Movements.* American Sociological Review, 62(5), 760–778. https://doi.org/10.2307/2657359

12. Election night 2018: *Historically high youth turnout, support for Democrats.* Circle at Tufts. (2018, November 7). https://circle.tufts.edu/latest-research/election-night-2018-historically-high-youth-turnout-support-democrats

13. Gao, G. (2020, May 30). *The up and down seasons of political campaign work.* Pew Research Center. https://www.pewresearch.org/short-reads/2014/11/17/the-seasonal-nature-of-political-campaign-work

14. The Democrats. (2019, February 21). *DNC Launches New Program: Organizing Corps 2020. Democrats News.* https://democrats.org/news/dnc-launches-new-program-organizing-corps-2020

15. U.S. Bureau of Labor Statistics. (2022, May 23). *61.8 percent of recent high school graduates enrolled in college in October 2021.* TED: The Economics Daily. https://www.bls.gov/opub/ted/2022/61-8-percent-of-recent-high-school-graduates-enrolled-in-college-in-october-2021.htm#:-:text=Bureau%20of%20Labor%20Statistics%2C%20U.S.,visited%20April%2028%2C%202023).

16. *Presidential candidates, 2020*. Ballotpedia. (n.d.). https://ballotpedia.org/Presidential.candidates, 2020

17. *List of registered 2020 presidential candidates*. Ballotpedia. (n.d.-a). https://ballotpedia.org-List.of.registered.2020.presidential.candidates#cite.note-6

18. Marsh, J. (2020, January 22). *Here's how Mike Bloomberg is luring 2020 campaign staffers with lavish perks*. New York Post. https://nypost.com/2020/01/22/heres-how-mike-bloomberg-is-luring-2020-campaign-staffers-with-lavish-perks

19. Center for American Women and Politics. (2023). *Gender differences in voter turnout*. Center for American Women and Politics, Eagleton Institute of Politics, Rutgers University-New Brunswick. https://cawp.rutgers.edu/facts/voters/gender-differences-voter-turnout

20. Balz, D. (2022, November 3). *Democrats count on huge black turnout, but has the party delivered in return?*. The Washington Post. https://www.washingtonpost.com/politics/interactive/2022/black-vote-elections-2022-democrats

21. WP Company. (2022, November 11). *Racial breakdowns for midterms expose shifting electorate*. The Washington Post. https://www.washingtonpost.com/nation/2022/11/11/black-asian-latino-voter-turnout

22. Goldberg, Z. (2023, February). *The Rise of College-Educated Democrats*. New York, New York; Manhattan Institute.

23. Tom Malinowski lost his seat as New Jersey's 7th Congressional District election in 2022 to the GOP candidate by approx 4.6%.

24. Moore, E. (2023, February 6). Gen Z's political power: New Data gives insight into America's youngest voters. NPR. https://www.npr.org/2023/02/06/1154172568/gen-zs-political-power-new-data-gives-insight-into-americas-youngest-voters

25. Griffiths, B. D. (2019, March 15). *Bernie Sanders' staffers unionize in first for presidential campaign*. Politico. https://www.politico.com/story/2019/03/15/bernie-campaign-2020-staff-union-1223914

26. Desai, S. (2019, August 24). *Why 2020 campaign workers are suddenly unionizing*. The Atlantic. https://www.theatlantic.com/politics/archive/2019/08/2020-campaigns-unionize-sanders-warren-booker-castro/596599

27. Axelrod, T. (2019, September 28). *Warren's campaign reaches tentative deal to unionize*. The Hill. https://thehill.com/homenews/campaign/463508-warren-campaign-reaches-tentative-union-deal

28. Weissert, W. (2023, March 23). *Pro-labor? Biden aims to prove it with unionized 2024 staff*. AP NEWS. https://apnews.com/article/biden-campaign-2024-union-labor-254d11b044a4bf2209ec434a702a1b96

29. Herrity, J. (2023, February 16). *Average salary in the US (with demographic data)*. Pay & Salary. https://www.indeed.com/career-advice/pay-salary/average-salary-in-us

Additional Reading and Resources

Involvement and Motivations

Auxier, B. (2020, July 13). *Activism on social media varies by race and ethnicity, age, political party*. Pew Research Center. https://www.pewresearch.org/short-reads/2020/07/13/activism-on-social-media-varies-by-race-and-ethnicity-age-political-party/

Cebul, M. (2023, January 20). *Youth activism: Balancing risk and reward*. United States Institute of Peace. https://www.printfriendly.com/p/g/KSzMCv

Harper, C., & National Center for Institutional Diversity We produce, catalyze, and elevate diversity research and scholarship. (2022, July 18). *College students, campus culture, and political participation*. https://medium.com/national-center-for-institutional-diversity/college-students-campus-culture-and-political-participation-17531dc7af38

Gampher, A. (2023, January 11). *Analysis: Q4 activism boosts 2022 activity to five-year high*. Bloomberg Law. https://news.bloomberglaw.com/bloomberg-law-analysis/analysis-q4-activism-boosts-2022-activity-to-five-year-high

Swing Blue Alliance. (2023, May 8). *Volunteer Results*. https://swingbluealliance.org/results

For Staffers

Guide to working on political campaigns. Harvard Law School. (2023, January 25). https://hls.harvard.edu/bernard-koteen-office-of-public-interest-advising/a-quick-guide-to-working-on-political-campaigns/

Political campaign worker. *Political Campaign Worker Careers | The Princeton Review*. (n.d.). https://www.princetonreview.com/careers/27/political-campaign-worker

Tulshyan, R. (2016, October 19). *What to do when you're called a "Diversity Hire."* Forbes. https://www.forbes.com/sites/ruchikatulshyan/2016/10/18/what-to-do-when-youre-called-a-diversity-hire

On diversity in politics

Abramowitz, A. I. (n.d.). *Sabato's Crystal Ball*. Sabatos Crystal Ball. https://centerforpolitics.org/crystalball/articles/both-white-and-nonwhite-democrats-are-moving-left/

Bleiweis, R., & Phadke, S. (2021, November 9). *The state of women's leadership-and how to continue changing the face of U.S. politics*. Center for American Progress. https://www.americanprogress.org/article/state-womens-leadership-continue-changing-face-u-s-politics/

Gothreau, C. (2020, October 9). *Revisiting the gender gap in 2020: The gender gap in political engagement*. Center for American Women and Politics . https://cawp.rutgers.edu/blog/revisiting-gender-gap-2020-gender-gap-political-engagement

Hakeemjefferson. (2021, May 10). How the politics of White Liberals and white conservatives are shaped by whiteness. FiveThirtyEight. https://fivethirtyeight.com/features/how-the-politics-of-white-liberals-and-white-conservatives-are-shaped-by-whiteness/

Unionizing on campaigns

Desai, S. (2019a, August 24). *Why 2020 campaign workers are suddenly unionizing*. The Atlantic. https://www.theatlantic.com/politics/archive/2019/08/2020-campaigns-unionize-sanders-warren-booker-castro/596599/

Weissert, W., & Miller, Z. (2023, March 23). *Pro-labor? Biden aims to prove it with unionized 2024 staff*. AP News. https://apnews.com/article/biden-campaign-2024-union-labor-254d11b044a4bf2209ec434a702a1b96#:.:text=Biden%27s%202020%20campaign%20only%20unionized,often%20dispatched%20to%20different%20states.

About the Author

Morgan Searcy is a creative lead, researcher, and strategist with a background in graphic design. Early on, Morgan worked in non-profit and branding spaces between Washington D.C. and Chicago. She supported design and creative strategy for two 2020 political campaigns: *Warren for President* and *Jon Ossoff for Senate*. Morgan also served as the Brand and Creative Director of *Rock the Vote*, leading digital initiatives that gained 61M+ organic impressions in the first two months. As a Co-Director, she is collaborating with *The People's Graphic Design Archive*, to promote equitable collection of histories.

One Year in Politics is an initiative of Morgan's global creative and consulting studio that provides long-term solutions through the lens of progressive values and concept-first approaches.

morgansearcy.com

Project
Credits

Special thanks to all the interviewees for your trust, Megha Bhattacharya and Davis Leonard, my Warren to Ossoff women, Kevin Lowery for listening to me talk about this project for almost 4 years, Leigh Kennedy for helping me spend the summer of 2017 in D.C., Suzy Smith, my first connection in politics, Raquel and Judy (and Elizabeth Warren) for hiring me, you don't know how much I needed it, Rock the Vote 2020 Team, and Jon Ossoff's digital team. The WHOLE Warren design team, ily forever. Many thanks to everyone who have supported me personally and professionally to share this body of work, thank you.

Interviewees: Nelowfar Ahmadi, Alex Ames, Caroline Beohm, Megha Bhattacharya, Liam Bodlak, Ethan Chase, Peter DeBaugh, Hannah Ezell, Hannah Gaffney, Luke Holey, Nicole Jevons, Kiera Manser, Kaitlyn May, Amelia Montooth, Marcus Nelson, Jade Ngengi, Megan Pappalardo, Gabbi Perry, Elliot Richardson, Jace Ritchey, Hazel Rosenblum-Sellers, Ellen Smith, Sojan Thrasher, Ezekiel Uriel, Natalie Valenzuela, Dawson Vandervort, Michael Watson, and others.

Data and project support: **Irina Alejandro**

Copy Editor: **Amy Schubert**

Reviewed by: **Raquel Breternitz, Kiayna O'Neal, Colleen Murphy, and Tim Norton**

Warren Design Team: Raquel Breternitz, Design Director, and design team Judy Su, Stacie Buelle, Eric Ziminsky, Victoria Adams, Riz Hernadaz, Julianna Egner, Molly Simon, Laura Porat, Grace Abe, and Colleen Murphy.

The Ossoff design and organizing teams; Heather Ellis, Jessica Lucia, Ezeke Uriel, Kiayna O'Neal, Elias Duncan, Julia Goldman, Kevin Lowery, and many others.

Photography Credits (page): Spurekar (cover), Kevin Lowery (48, 108), Jorge Alcala (42), Michael Amadeus (93), Israel Andrade (79), Clay Banks (54), Manny Becerra (94), Brooke Cagl (211), Compare Fibre (90), Cottonbro Studio (16), Nathan Dumlao (24, 39, 101), Jeffery Erhunse (66), Etty Fidele (58), Aiony Haust Mche Lee (36), Library of Congress (60), Monstera Production (63), Tom Morbey (51), Sushil Nash (209), Josue Ladoo Pelegrin (89), Danzel Gian Mabiling Sepillo (86), Gage Skidmore (73), Annie Spratt (74, 76), Ketut Subiyanto (80), Polina Tankilevitc (66), Vlad Tchompalov (116), Josue Verdejo (63), Duané Viljoen (34), Joe Yates (34), Wan San Yip (105)

Design & Creative: Morgan Searcy, Joan Comellas
Typefaces: *Editorial New* & *Acumin Concept*
Printed in USA

For more information, to book an event, or inquire about special discounts for bulk purchases, please contact **hello@politicsproject.com** and visit **politicsproject.com**